The Workplace Community

A Guide to Releasing Human Potential and Engaging Employees

Ian Gee

*International OD Consultant, Owner Edgelands
Consultancy and Co Founder Albany OD, UK*

Matthew Hanwell

*Former HR Director, Communities & Social Media, Nokia,
Finland*

First published 2014 by
PALGRAVE MACMILLAN

Palgrave Macmillan in the UK is an imprint of Macmillan Publishers Limited,
registered in England, company number 785998, of Houndmills, Basingstoke,
Hampshire RG21 6XS.

Palgrave Macmillan in the US is a division of St Martin's Press LLC,
175 Fifth Avenue, New York, NY 10010.

Palgrave Macmillan is the global academic imprint of the above companies
and has companies and representatives throughout the world.

Palgrave® and Macmillan® are registered trademarks in the United States,
the United Kingdom, Europe and other countries.

ISBN 978–1–137–44167–6

This book is printed on paper suitable for recycling and made from fully
managed and sustained forest sources. Logging, pulping and manufacturing
processes are expected to conform to the environmental regulations of the
country of origin.

A catalogue record for this book is available from the British Library.

Library of Congress Cataloging-in-Publication Data

Gee, Ian Robert, 1959-

The workplace community : a guide to releasing human potential and engaging
employees / Ian Gee, International OD Consultant, Edgelands Consultancy, UK,
Matthew Hanwell, Former HR Director, Communities & Social media, Nokia.

pages cm.—(Palgrave pocket consultants)

Summary: "Most organizations are laced with communities that cut through and across
departments and levels of hierarchy. However they often remain small, invisible and
hampered by a lack of explicit support and license. In an increasingly knowledge-based
economy, what we know, our thoughts, ideas, creativity, innovation and our willingness
to share and collaborate, are critical for creating value for organisations and the
individuals who work for them, and organisations are seeking ways of emulating the
innovation and passion found present in start-ups and with entrepreneurs. Workplace
communities provide a way to tap into this collective intelligence, engage people in a
common sense of direction and provide the opportunity for unleashing 'intrepreneurship'
across the organisation. The Workplace Community offers a structured, practical guide
for understanding and developing creative and effective communities in the workplace,
from introducing employees and managers to new ways of working, to measuring
effectiveness and providing corrective interventions for those who haven't achieved the
desired results."—Provided by publisher.

ISBN 978–1–137–44167–6   (paperback)
1. Employee motivation.   2. Business communication.   3. Organizational change.
I. Hanwell, Matthew.   II. Title.
HF5549.5.M63G44 2014
658.3'14—dc23   2014026515

Typeset by MPS Limited, Chennai, India.

Matthew:
Dedicated to my wife Mari-Hanna
and children: Emma, Thomas, Johanna, Katie and Sophie

Ian:
Dedicated to my parents, Bill and Barbara Gee
and my partner Robert Priestley

Contents

List of Figures and Tables

Figures

Tables

Preface

We approached the writing of this book after having both worked in multiple organizations, large and small, private and public sector as well as not for profit. We have had various roles in organizations including Organization Development (OD) for a combined 50+ years! We will draw on this experience, which includes being both internal and external consultants.

We have considerable experience of initiating, supporting and diagnosing the issues workplace communities face and will draw, in a very practical way, on a range of disciplines including sociology, psychology and anthropology as well as business management and leadership development. Our primary focus is enabling organizations of all types to achieve their desired outcomes through making a conscious choice as to how to organize the way they work.

Our interest in workplace communities became more focussed while we both were working for Nokia Corp. Ian was Director of Organization Development and Matthew was HR Director of Communities and Social Media. We were asked to bring our expertise to bear on a project to review Nokia's ways of working. It was an invitation to question the status quo, to investigate how work was being performed, to challenge how an organization accomplishes its business objectives, and an invitation to experiment and to develop.

At the heart of this was the need to develop appropriate ways of challenging the organization to think about how work was performed and to raise awareness of the different choices that existed. The aim being to create an opportunity for leaders and employees to pause and challenge themselves as to whether or not hierarchy, the most common way of organizing in Nokia, as in most organizations, was appropriate to the tasks in hand.

At Nokia we identified four different ways of working: line mode, project mode, investment mode and finally community mode. As well as helping to develop thinking and practice in all of the modes, while others focussed their efforts on the other modes we concentrated on community ways of working. For us this was the least explored way of working and we believed it offered the greatest potential for innovation, creativity and engagement.

There is much research, writing and good practice in the field of community development. However, the majority of this is focussed on the communities we live in and in particular support for disadvantaged communities and those practitioners wishing to bring about social change. This is good work and we have learnt a lot from it. What we found missing, however, was how to bring the benefits of community into the workplace. In essence, how to make the changes in organizations that allow these benefits to be replicated inside the enterprise.

This book is a practical handbook and provides you the reader with straightforward and easy to understand ways to initiate and develop a workplace community. It contains examples as well as easy to use pragmatic frameworks, tools and models. In terms of success measures, we have developed a scorecard that businesses and workplace communities can use to follow the activity levels within their communities, understand the value community is creating for its members and track the business impact and outcomes – the community performance. After reading this book, we believe you will find it easy to decide if a workplace community is right for your organization and have the tools, techniques and confidence to sell the idea to those who have the ability to say yes!

Acknowledgments

We would like to thank everyone who has helped us both directly and indirectly with this book. This includes all those people who we have been in a workplace community with. It is only a shame that there are too many of you to mention! We both learnt a tremendous amount from you all and without your inspiration this book would not have ever come into being.

There are also a number of people we would like specifically to thank for their contribution to our writing and thinking. This has included sharing your thoughts and ideas as well as providing comments on the manuscript as we developed it.

We are very grateful for the support of the following friends who provided us with feedback on individual chapters. Thanks to your input the book is much better than it would have been.

Dee Ortner
David Stoneham
Amanda Gartshore
Satu Teerkangas
Natalia Bogoyavlenskaya
Asif Zulfiqar
Tojo Eapen

Thank you Tine Huus and Pierre Ouellet for letting us develop and use the 'Ways of Working Questionnaire' you jointly worked on.

Tine Huus deserves a further mention for her expert advice and support in developing the Chapter 'Metrics and Meaning'.

Thank you as well to Wilson Wong, for initiating contact with the publishers and reviewing our original proposal.

And finally and by no means least we would like to thank our families and friends for putting up with us being out of commission for the last few months and locked in our studies writing away! We could not have done it without you!

chapter 1

Introduction

Welcome to the world of workplace communities!

Our aim in writing this book is to introduce you to the world of workplace communities. All of us are familiar with the idea of social communities, whether it is a club of some kind we belong to, either physically or virtually, or the local community we live in. Communities are one of the oldest ways of organizing and getting things done. People coming together and organizing around something that is important to them. A place where they feel their contribution is valued and can make a difference. Contrast this with most of today's organizations, where people organize around hierarchy and annually defined tasks and targets, working to fixed, often outdated, job descriptions.

Most companies carry out some form of annual or biannual staff survey, and in the majority of cases leaders and managers spend time pondering why the 'holy grail' of employee engagement cannot be found in their workplace. We believe that consciously and actively developing communities inside the workplace, which are organized around what matters to people, is a way of overcoming this. This book will show you how to do this. To identify if and when a community approach is right for you, the steps you can take to introduce one and how to support, develop and enable it so everyone can reap the rewards community ways of working can bring.

Target audience

Our target audience for this book is leaders, managers and employees. If you are a leader or a manager who senses or knows there is something beyond hierarchy but you are struggling to find it, someone who truly wishes to unleash the latent potential within their organization, and to reach new levels of engagement and performance, then this book is for you. If you are an employee who feels your current ways of working are not enabling you to contribute in ways you know you would like, and you want to find other ways of working, then this book is for you. It will give you the support you need to open up discussions with your leaders and managers and help you to work with them to explore the possibilities and create the opportunities to achieve more together.

Tomorrow's workplace today?

As you read this book we ask you to imagine a workplace where people are not bound by departmental barriers, a place where employees feel a commitment to the whole organization and not just their separate silo. Employees who see the organization 'in the round' and know where their contribution could make a difference, despite this being not part of their job description or annual tasks and targets. The kind of workplace where people feel such a strong sense of community that being a partisan is not an option. Workplaces where fiefdoms and territorial conflicts are consider things of the past and to be laughed at! This is the kind of workplace that a community way of working can bring you. An organization where people feel their contribution is not bounded by their role but is open and expressive across the whole of the organization. Where people feel a commitment to not just their own tasks, targets and outcomes but those of the whole organization.

By workplace communities, we do not mean people sitting around in a circle fighting over who is going to get the talking stick next! We mean, a structured and planned way by which people have the opportunity to contribute and work outside of the traditional hierarchy and silos of organization. Engaging with each other in very different ways and in doing so creating extraordinary results. We believe workplace communities, if implemented with diligence and care, can unleash latent talent, capability and capacity in the organization and have a positive impact on business results.

We believe that developing and supporting workplace communities provides any organization, private, public or not for profit, with the opportunity to deliver excellent business results and at the same time provide the kind of environment where people can do the best work of their lives.

Engagement and contribution

Giving people the opportunity to be part of a thriving workplace community not only increases their engagement and commitment to the organization as a whole but also helps them develop their skills and capabilities. In some cases these will be new skills and abilities, but in many cases they are skills and capabilities that, although active in employees' lives outside of work, remain dormant and not accessed in the workplace. We believe that recognizing this will help you to reshape your current ways of working and help you secure the future success of your organization. By following the practical guidance offered in this book you will be able to move beyond traditional organizational boundaries and ways of working and unleash the pent up creative passion and excitement of both your employees and yourself.

Default position

Have you ever asked yourself why the way we organize work has not changed? If you have, then this book is for you! Many of us work very differently from our parents' and grandparents' generations. That is, we don't necessarily go to the office, factory or mine every day. We work remotely and increasingly in a global context with higher levels of autonomy. What has not changed however is the structure of work. Hierarchy is still the dominant way of organizing how we contribute to the enterprise, how we manage and how we get recognized and rewarded for our contributions. There is nothing inherently wrong with hierarchy. It certainly has its benefits when properly instigated. However as a 'default position' for organizing we believe that it has outlived its usefulness. By 'default position' we mean we automatically make this choice without thinking or considering what other options might be available. We may not even know or understand that we have other choices as to how we work.

One way of thinking about this is to think about your computer. When you switch it on it automatically defaults to its 'C' drive and if you want to work on another drive you have to make a conscious choice, enter the computer's settings and choose that drive you want. Most organizations cannot think of any other way of getting work done other than with an organizational chart that shows where you 'sit' in the hierarchy, job descriptions that define roles and responsibilities and employees contained, we would argue and constrained, by both.

Hierarchy has its place in the organization, for example the organization of routine tasks and activities or when work requires absolute structure and precision. Here is an example, when the fire service responds to a 'shout' having a clear command and control structure is essential. Firefighters, men and women, need to be clear on their roles and responsibilities and know when and how to respond to commands. Similarly hospital emergency rooms rely on a clear and understood hierarchy to save lives, likewise, the military. Ask yourself, how often in today's businesses do we need to operate like the military or emergency services?

In our view hierarchy should be a positive choice and not a default. Overused, hierarchy drives out creativity and the opportunity for the unexpected to bring innovation and the possibility of positive difference. In the organization context it makes sense to use hierarchy to organize say payroll or compliance services. These are areas of business that rely on certainty and predictability. They are repetitive activities in which variation needs to be planned, controlled, monitored and recorded. However we would argue that well over 75 percent of the work of most organizations does not necessarily require hierarchy as the dominant organization form. Hierarchy may be sufficient to get the job done, but it may not actually be necessary. By making hierarchy a default position we drive out the possibility of getting much better outcomes and results and of raising the engagement of employees.

Sector specific?

The potential for implementing and developing a workplace community that delivers excellent results is not sector specific. There may be differences in how you approach the job of engaging people, leaders and employees with the ideas contained in this book and how you manage your current governance structure. How you measure success in terms of outcomes may also differ. But the basic principles remain the same. This book will guide you as to how to have the discussions you need to be persuasive and stimulate thinking about the possibilities and potential that workplace communities can offer your organization.

Not only do we believe that the current workforce is looking for new ways of working and achieving but we also know from our research that the new generations entering the workplace, Gen Y or the Net Gen, are looking for a different relationship to work, one that is not bounded by the traditions of those that have gone before them. We are increasingly working in a multigenerational, digital, knowledge-based, global workplace – enabled by Internet and social media. A lot of research has shown that the new generations entering the workplace expect and demand a different experience of the workplace from earlier generations. They have grown up with the web and associated technology and are expecting to experience the kind of freedoms and opportunities for both business and personal achievement that this provides.

In our experience, most organizations are laced with communities; however these may remain small, often invisible and hampered by a lack of explicit support and license. In the increasingly knowledge-based economy, what we know, our thoughts, ideas, creativity, innovation and our willingness to share and collaborate, are critical for creating value for organizations and the individuals who work for them.

Many progressive organizations are seeking ways of emulating the innovation and passion found in startups and the work of entrepreneurs. Developing a workplace community provides a way for older, more established organizations to tap into this collective intelligence, engage people in a common sense of direction and provide the opportunity for unleashing 'intrepreneurship' across the organization. Most entrepreneurs tend to favor community ways of working during their startup stage. This is often stimulated and supported by the innovation hubs in which they work, and which, by their very design, encourage cross-pollination and the sharing of ideas and approaches. It is only as they develop and start to formalize their ways of working that hierarchy becomes the default. When we have talked to entrepreneurs they often speak wistfully about the excitement and creativity that was present at the start of their work and how they seem to have lost this as they grow bigger and start to institutionalize their processes and ways of working.

Not by accident

Workplace communities do not come about by accident; they require intentionality. In this book we will provide you with a clear definition of a workplace community and ideas as to when this is best applied. We will explain how to initiate one, how to map the developmental stages they naturally go through, what to do if your community gets trapped at a particular stage of development and how to measure its effectiveness.

If you do already have a workplace community in place, then this book will give you the tools and techniques you need to help it flourish. We will also provide you with easy-to-use ways of measuring and reporting its effectiveness. If your community has got a bit 'stuck' we will provide you with an easy-to-use diagnostic approach, and pragmatic corrective interventions.

Workplace communities are not the 'holy grail' of organization – that is something we will all be searching for, for the rest of our lives! But this book will provide you with the opportunity to shift your own thinking and that of your organization and it will provide you with the opportunity take a new and fresh look at how you think about work and what outcomes really matter.

chapter 2

Ways of Working

Introduction

In this chapter we will explore the different ways of working that exist and help you determine if and when a particular way of working is most appropriate to what you are trying to accomplish. Through this exploration we hope that you will begin to see that how we execute work is a choice rather than simply a given, or as we prefer to call it, a 'default position'. That is, we always choose one way over another regardless of whether it will work or not.

At the end of this chapter we will introduce you to a tool we have co-developed, the 'Ways of Working Diagnostic Tool'. This tool will help you explore the choices that are available to you in relation to the task you wish to undertake.

There is nothing inherently right or wrong with any of the ways of working described in this chapter. None is better than the other. We hope to encourage you to make a conscious choice and in doing so to pick the way of working that is most likely to lead to success, in terms of the task in hand and also for those who you are asking to engage with it.

Finally, we hope this chapter will help you when talking with stake-holders about setting up a workplace community. By understanding and being familiar with different ways of working, their benefits and drawbacks, you can help people think through why your idea of initiating a workplace community is the best way of achieving a successful outcome.

SCENARIO

Imagine you have been called in to see your boss. Your organization is doing very well and has ambitious plans to expand into new markets. There is an ever-growing demand for its products and services outside of the home territory. However this expansion has not been without its problems. The dreams and passion that headquarters has for developing organizational excellence, and at the same time generating ethical profits, has not been fully realised. No one seems to know why. Demand is now rising in SE Asia and the organization's senior leaders are very keen to open offices across the region. It wants to build a strong and successful presence. In addition to market opportunities, HR have identified that SE Asia could provide the organization with a rich source of much-needed talent. Given the bumpy entry the organization has had into other new markets, the CEO commissioned a couple of quick and dirty studies to find out what has worked and what has not worked. But having read through these and talked to a few people, you are still not much clearer on what the organization is missing and not getting right. Your boss has asked you to lead this market entry and to make sure that it happens quickly, smoothly and becomes a model that the company to use for future such initiatives. So what do you do?

Do you go and find the 'usual suspects' and set up a short-life project team to work with you?

Do you work through the hierarchy, as a sole contributor, trying to influence and direct things. Using your natural enthusiasm and any expert power you have? If needs be, drawing on the authority of your boss to get things done?

Do you tell your boss that, given the growing importance of the new market entry and that there are many other new markets that the organization will want to enter in the next couple of years or so, you need to set up a new department called 'Market Entry', get HR to produce job descriptions, have them evaluated and then recruit to them from inside and outside the organization looking for the best in the field. To get the best you will also need to pay the best and will need to develop an attractive bonus scheme to ensure appropriate reward and manage retention. Of course you will be the new senior vice-president of Market Entry and will need to sit down with your boss to define tasks and targets, key performance indicators (KPIs), a vision and mission statement and agree a strategy. You will also need to create an organization chart. In addition there will need to be some discussion about office space, location and technology for the new department.

So what do you choose to do? What option most attracts you? What do you think will work best for the organization, employees, and of course for yourself? How do you make the choice? Is it a conscious one or do you just roll up your sleeves and get on with it?

Thinking about our ways of working

The vast majority of us take for granted that the way work is performed and the way we are managed is the way it always has been, and perhaps, how it always will and should be! {*Or we hate it but don't say anything, or we don't think about it at all because we don't understand the benefit of having the right way of working (WoW)*}

When we first enter the workplace, we follow the established policies, practices and procedures that have most likely served the organization for years and years. We accept the status quo; probably our first manager will help with the induction process, showing us the ropes. Helping us to understand how things are 'done around here'. Naturally we want to fit in and so we accept things as they are. Most likely these established ways of getting things done haven't changed that much from the first day that your manager entered the workplace, or your manager's manager for that matter. They were likely to have been inducted in the same way by their first manager and so on down the ages. The baton of ways of working is passed on and becomes the way we do things with little questioning as to what else might be possible.

This is amazing when you start to consider the major technological, mobile, and social advances that we have experienced in our working lifetimes. Not to mention the effects of digitalization and globalization impacting almost every aspect of our business, commercial and personal worlds. Frederick Taylor, known for being the father of scientific management, would recognize many of the working practices of today in the majority of organizations, even though he died in 1915!

Many of the working practices we hold dear were developed and first implemented during the early industrial era. They aimed to optimize productivity at a time when most workers used their hands to produce material goods or grow agricultural produce.

> It is only through enforced standardization of methods, enforced adoption of the best implements and working conditions, and enforced cooperation that this faster work can be assured. And the duty of enforcing the adoption of standards and enforcing this cooperation rests with management alone. (Taylor F, *Principles of Scientific Management*, 1911)

This reflects Taylor's principles and practices of management more than a century ago. Today, these practices remain prevalent in hierarchical organizations and management systems, although concepts such as employee engagement reflect more of the voluntary nature of effort than the strict enforcement to which Taylor refers.

Leaders and managers have a significant influence on the ways of working within the organization. The personal goals and aspirations of leaders and managers together with their experience of what works will drive them towards their default position, their preferred way of getting things done. Often they will simply impose this on their organization and teams without pausing for thought. While a manager may want to encourage openness, engagement and participation as part of a way of working, it may be that the task at hand dictates a specific way of working – perhaps a project approach. Leaders and managers are typically very busy; they may lack the skills or knowledge to appreciate the benefits of different ways of working, and the thought of losing control may drive fear and uncertainty in them. The individual goals and agenda of leaders and managers will significantly influence ways of working.

We now live in the post-industrial era often referred to as the digital or internet age. Many of the people within our organizations work with knowledge, ideas, thoughts and concepts. In this predominantly 'knowledge-based economy' it is the extent to which knowledge is shared, processed and utilized, to drive innovations and differentiation in products and services, that creates value for organizations. For many in the workforce, it is no longer about how many widgets they can produce in an hour.

Given that this revolution is already happening and will continue to happen, we believe it is time to reconsider our ways of working. If we don't, we suspect that the competitiveness of many organizations will diminish as the more forward-thinking, nimble, and agile take advantage of and benefit from the possibilities of new ways working.

As of early 2014, 52 percent of the Fortune 500 firms since 2000 are gone! (Marion Kaufman Foundation Research 2014)

Time to reconsider?

When you start to consider how work is done and how organizations continually evolve and develop, you will soon see that there are distinct and very different ways of working. Some of these ways of working are appropriate for some industries and certain sectors. Others have evolved over time, being driven by a perceived need to improve collaboration and coordination.

Most enterprises are started by a small number of people, perhaps one or two, who have a business idea that they want to develop. With such small numbers of people involved, roles and responsibilities don't need to be very specific. The individuals concerned can agree who does what, even on a daily basis, as needs and tasks demand. This can easily shift and change over time with people picking up or dropping tasks as required. An enterprise may never develop, or even want to develop beyond this size. A small family-run business, a restaurant or a shop, is an example of this. Such small enterprises will have an intimate understanding of their customers and will have the flexibility to respond to any new customer demands, within their capabilities. Not everyone is looking to establish a chain or build an empire!

Regardless of the size of the organization, there will be known and recognized tasks to be performed and some specialist skills needed to perform them. However, in general, there will be fluidity in the way resources are used. With people being willing to multitask and recognizing the need to take on roles from time to time that are outside to their comfort zone. Communication will be immediate and normally face-to-face, with people in these small enterprises usually being located in the same place (co-located). There will be a limited management system in place and if additional resources are needed, say for a specific period of time, there will be an informal process to bring these in. This may be a family friend, a relative or someone who knows someone who can help! There will be a leader who makes the decisions.

As the enterprise grows, there will be the need to add more resources, more people, to fuel this growth. With this growth comes a separation of roles and responsibilities and an increasing need for specialists to perform specific and/or functional tasks. As the enterprise scales up, there is a need for more organization, more structure and the need for a management system that will allocate and control resources. At some point someone will draw an organizational chart! Something to help people understand who is where and who does what!

Assuming the enterprise remains successful and as it continues to scale up, there will be the need for additional communication and information. This is to ensure that all parts of the enterprise are kept informed and aware of what is currently happening and of future possibilities. Specialist functions will start to emerge like R&D, Communications, Finance, Human Resources, Marketing and Production. The people who perform these specialist roles will be organized to perform the specific function or sub-function as needed. Such functions will develop themselves to optimize their own capabilities and their perceived role in the value chain of the organization. Once again as the enterprise continues to grow these functional areas will continue to expand and develop further.

At some point it will be realized that silos have appeared. It is not that anyone builds walls around the specific functional areas, however boundaries and borders will have emerged. These boundaries will likely start to inhibit cooperation and collaboration. In many cases the various functional areas will be competing for the same resources of the organization. They will also start competing for attention, wanting to assert their authority and exercise their power. This can become extremely dysfunctional – like the liver competing with the kidneys and spleen in the human body!

Of course leaders of organizations will recognize this, measures will be taken to minimize the negative effects, and perhaps a matrix organization will be introduced to ensure multiple lines of responsibility and reduce the silo behavior. And so on and so on!

Large and complex organizations can find it challenging to remain aware and sensitive to customer and market changes. There will typically be several functions that interface with the 'customer' such as customer services, professional services, sales, and so on, and the ability to pull and willingness to share information across these functions will be a challenge. Unlike the small enterprise, it will also be challenging to respond quickly to a new customer need or demand. It may even be difficult to know who can make the decision across the various organizational boundaries. In addition it is likely that product and service life cycles will have become extended. So even if a new customer need is known, introducing this into the already full three-year road map, which has been approved by the chain of command, may be difficult or even impossible. If you work in a large, complex organization, imagine if a representative of your largest customer were to call you today, and say that the ten thousand widgets they had ordered in red, they now wanted in black, and could you still deliver on time? How would you respond? Who would you call? How long would it take for your organization to decide if this was even possible? More importantly how would your response and the time it took to respond, impact on your largest customer's sense of satisfaction?

Over the years, organizations have employed numerous consultants and spent countless amounts of money looking for the holy grail of organization. This is most often a search for excellence in terms of a fixed world view of how organizations should be organized and the way we believe work should be conducted.

Four ways of working

We have identified four ways of working, some of which you will no doubt be more familiar with than others. No single one of them is better or worse than the others. What we want you to be able to do is think about what would work best when, and which way of working will provide you with the results you are looking for. Rather than simply and automatically default to the one you are most familiar with, which will most likely be hierarchy!

The four ways of working are (1) the hierarchical organization, (2) the program/project approach, (3) entrepreneurism/intrapreneurism, and (4) workplace communities. We will outline and benefits and limitations of the first three. The fourth alternative Community Ways of Working is of course the focus of this book.

Hierarchical

The hierarchical organization is the most common way of working and the one we are all most familiar with. It is highly likely that you may have never experienced anything other than being part of a hierarchy. Hierarchy is characterized by a command and control approach. In this section we will explore when this is the most appropriate way of working and when it is not. As you read this section hold in mind Charlie Chaplin's famous 1936 film, *Modern Times*!

Hierarchical, line-structured organizations are good and achieve results when your objectives include:

• Scale
• Rigor and efficiency
• Structured growth
• Command and control – getting things done
• Repeatable execution
• Cost efficiencies
• Predictability
• Managing anxiety – as everyone knows what is expected of them.

In a successful hierarchy everyone knows their place and understands what is expected of them. They know who they report to and how to report. They know the boundaries of their roles and when to pass things up or down the organization for decision-making or action. Employees know and understand the scope of their authority and what they are responsible for. They have fixed job descriptions and usually have annual tasks and targets, which are reviewed by their immediate superior.

Employees are recruited on the basis of specific skills that match the needs of the role. Their reward and compensation is fixed, with job descriptions being evaluated for comparative worth and levels of complexity.

Hierarchies are usually represented diagrammatically as some form of pyramid with one person at the top and with layers broadening out beneath. Relationships between the layers are controlled and managed. To coordinate between different parts of the hierarchy things move up to the highest point of commonality and then down the line to where the action needs to occur.

The specific benefits of a hierarchical way of working include:

- Clarity on who is in charge – authority is obvious and employees know who to turn to, and how to ask for decisions to keep things moving forward
- Leaders, managers and employees are recognized as having specific skills. The organization recruits for these skills and capabilities and they are usually expressed clearly in an employee's job title along with indicating their position in the hierarchy
- It is usually clear how you advance and 'get on' in a hierarchy. Promotion pathways are publicized and normally based on merit as well as the demonstration of skills. Employees are encouraged to aspire to the next level in the hierarchy and often supported in their development to be ready for this. This leads to a regular flow of home grown talent with employees moving up the organization
- Hierarchies develop a loyalty in the employees who often truly identify with their department.

Hierarchies are good at what they do. On the down side they are:

- Rigid, fixed and do not encourage flexibility
- Slow to respond to change
- Limit creativity by over-managing the free flow of information. In turn this can disable innovation and engagement
- Information accuracy can be compromised when people have to pass messages through a number of layers to get to the point where decisions can be made
- They can create dependency and reduce personal agency. Employees become so dependent on their superiors defining reality that they lose the ability to make sense of things for themselves. For this same reason they can stifle creativity as creativity tends only to be encouraged within the boundaries of an employee's position and role
- People know their place and are encouraged to stay in it unless they choose to apply and get selected for another role.

As previously stated, hierarchy is the most common form of organization and has served businesses well over the years. It is important to understand that it is not the only way of working and that we too often default into it. We create pyramids and hierarchies when other possibilities exist and may be cheaper, more effective and better places for employees to work.

Program and project

> A project is an endeavour in which human, financial and material resources are organized in a novel way to undertake a unique scope of work, of given specification, within constraints of cost and time, so as to achieve beneficial change or value defined by quantitative and qualitative objectives.
>
> A program of projects is a group of projects that contribute to a common, higher order objective. (*Handbook of Project-based Management* by J Rodney Turner, 2009)

An organization working in 'program mode' has adapted its operational mode and ways of working. That is, its people and organization; management system and leadership practices; processes and behaviors, in a way that it is capable of successfully and sustainably *creating value* by running a portfolio of projects and programs.

The program way of working means that an organization is able to resource, mobilize and prioritize programs and projects that are truly cross-functional. They have access to the diverse skills, knowledge and experiences that people have regardless of their hierarchical or functional position.

This way of working helps organizations source people from the various functional areas. It provides a framework for how these people will interface and collaborate from their given roles for the duration of their involvement in the project. By definition, projects are temporary, they start, they execute, they deliver an outcome and then they end.

Projects and programs are excellent ways of working when:

- What needs to be done is clearly understood
- The tasks can be logically broken down in to work packages and sequenced over time
- There is a specific scope and outcome
- There is a given timeframe, resources and budget.

There are many benefits of working in a project and/or program mode, these include:

• Bringing order and structure to otherwise uncoordinated activities and to schedule these in time, based upon dependencies.
• Aligning and focussing efforts for a common outcome or deliverable.
• Allowing needed skills and competencies to be resourced from various parts of an organization
• Providing cross-organizational visibility to activities through a well-managed portfolio.
• Creating a common language through the use of a methodology, and consistent criteria at key decision points or milestones.
• Fostering cross-functional knowledge and interaction
• Generating a sense of commitment towards the goal/deliverables and often building team spirit for the duration of the project.
• Focussing energy and effort to get things done with speed, precision, and engagement.

Programs and projects are not without their challenges, these include:

• Achieving continuity and a sense of long-term accountability beyond the life of the project
• Redundant overheads and excessive lead times when applied to what are in essence, simple tasks or activities – it doesn't make sense to try to apply a project approach to absolutely everything you do in an organization
• Poor at supporting formal on-the-job learning. Typically a project will need the required competence/skill to be fully available according to the project schedule, while the task is performed, and the resource then released when no longer needed. In circumstances like this there is not much time for skill development
• Accountability for knowledge and talent management. This is normally the responsibility of the line manager
• Ambiguous sense of belonging in the organization, 'I'm committed to the project that I have been assigned to, however my professional alliance is with my functional organization'

- Lack of clear career paths – it is unclear how performing roles within projects, over time, will result in a promotion or further a career as in a hierarchical organization
- Fairness of performance evaluations – to what extent do the performance management processes take into account the contribution made to a project?
- Territorialism entering the project world – trying to make your project look better than it is or protecting the projects that are sponsored by your part of the organization.
- Project fatigue especially for projects that have an extended timeline. Project members and even the wider organization can lose sight of the project purpose, which may no longer be valid.
- Shortage of experienced project managers – many projects are not completed successfully on time, at cost, and with quality because of poor project/program management.

In program and/or project mode, individuals assigned to projects will find a new form of relationship. In the formal organization they are used to having a line manager. This will be the person who hires and fires them, coaches them, sets their goals and objectives, provides feedback, reviews their tasks and targets on an annual basis and determines their compensation level. In a project they now have a relationship with the project manager. The project manager will have expectations of them and will monitor their contribution to the project, though they are unlikely to care much about the individuals' long-term development or career aspirations! Project managers will have little influence on overall career progression and compensation. The balance and clarity between the line manager and the project manager is important so as not to confuse the individual employee.

The first time you work in a project, you can have very mixed feelings. Your functional area has been your 'home', a place where the people around you speak the same language and talk about the same topics. You will most likely have a strong sense of comfort and stability. You may also feel considerable loyalty to your boss and fellow workers. You understand the rules and how to get things done. In the project world, you are joining a new team, a 'short life organisation' only brought together for the duration of the project. The other members will most likely come from different functional areas, some of which you may never have heard of! This can generate feelings of insecurity and concerns about fellow project teammates' expectations of you. You may also spend time wondering where support will come from. It will take time for the project team to form and develop together the relationships and ways of working needed for success. Project teams classically go through Bruce Tuckman's cycle of 'forming, norming, storming and performing'. (*Developmental Sequences in Small Groups*, 1965)

There are many project/program methodologies. These include blueprints for how to run a successful project. Many of us will have seen WBSs (Work Breakdown Structures), Gantt charts, Pert charts, and Critical Path Analyses, as well as costing, risk management, and other tracking processes that need to be applied to get work done in a project mode.

More recently, 'agile' and 'lean' methodologies and approaches have been applied to projects. This brings new ways of working and interacting into programmes and projects, for example, scrum teams, backlogs, sprints, iterations and so on. Agile project approaches provide a more nimble way of working over the traditional 'waterfall' approach, where progress typically flows from top to bottom like a cascading waterfall. This can cause confusion to stakeholders not familiar with the concepts and not least because they generally prioritize individuals and interactions over processes and tools! Agile and lean approaches have been widely applied in software engineering projects and are now increasingly being applied to non-technological projects.

In many cases and situations projects and project management methodologies are the primary way of working, for example, in building construction. They are particularly common in any work that has a logical and sequenced set of activities and with resources in need of coordination over time.

There are challenges with projects, in particular how projects and programs are run within the context of an organization.

The first challenge with projects and programs is that they are exclusive. Meaning only the people who have been allocated to a specific project role are involved and can contribute. You can't just turn up to a project team uninvited with a good idea or a solution and throw it into the project. Typically projects have their own resourcing mechanisms, they are able secure the resources and skills they need for the duration of the project. At the end of the project, the resources are returned to the organization from whence they came, as the project has ended and they are no longer needed.

In organizations where a lot of work is performed as projects, it is not uncommon for the people with the most valuable skills to be 'allocated' to multiple projects. Unfortunately this can result in people being spread thinly, perhaps having 5 percent of their time allocated to project A, 15 percent to project B, a further 10 percent to project C, and so on. They may also still be required to keep their 'day job' alive as well! In reality this means they will most likely spend all of their allocated project time catching up with what the project is doing and contributing very little of any real added value. Their day job will most likely suffer as well. In addition they are highly likely to feel distracted and disappointed not to be contributing fully to the projects they are engaged with or making a difference with their day jobs.

Projects and programs are not always the best way for us to organize our work, in particular when projects and programs are running within the hierarchical structures of the wider organization. In cases like these, leaders of the wider organization retain responsibility for the deliverables and outcome of the project or program, so they will naturally want to be part of the governance structure. It will also be likely that the project/programs resources will come from the same hierarchical organization, so once again the relevant line managers will want control over what their people are doing. They are the ones giving the project 'their' resources, from 'their' cost center. The line manager will also control the objective-setting and later performance review of 'their' people. Consequently, you can end up with projects or programs lacking the flexibility they need to move quickly, and being overly hidebound by trying to manage the concerns and anxieties of their multiple sponsors.

Running projects within the organization's functional silos, where there is a common chain of command is easier. Running cross-functional projects and programs requires a greater level of leadership maturity, where leaders think of the whole organization and what is good for it and not only about what is good for their own team or department. Unfortunately in our experience these broader goals are rarely included in a leader's annual objectives. Hence, there is little incentive for them to think holistically.

Let's highlight this dilemma with a case example:

A senior leader was sponsoring a companywide initiative to improve the company intranet. The existing intranet was fragmented and disjointed; it had been constructed from various parts, and had little consistency; in effect, a mirror of the organization. There were clear pain points to be addressed, a business case and clear deliverables that would make a significant difference for everyone in the organization. For the project to be successful, it would need the contribution and participation of people from several other parts of the organization. The goal was to bring consistency to the user experience and to provide common intranet services to employees and managers that crossed organizational boundaries. The people and commitment needed were from different functional areas and were therefore not under the leader's direct control. The project proposal was presented to the head of one of the other organizations. They agreed that it was indeed a great idea, that it should certainly be done, and that the organization would benefit. But unfortunately they were not able to commit any resources, due to them having their own project portfolio and completely separate priorities and portfolio governance! The project proceeded without other parts of the organization. Unsurprisingly it was only able to achieve limited success.

Entrepreneurial and intrapreneurial

Our third way of working draws on the world of entrepreneurs and startups. Many organizations are seeking to encourage the growth of entrepreneurial behavior within their workplace.

They are calling this, by what we consider to be a rather awkward term, intrapreneurship. By this they mean seeking to replicate, inside the enterprise, the working conditions and ways of working that make an entrepreneur successful. Organizations see this as a way of unleashing energy, effort, talent and creativity. The kind of creativity, innovation and passion they see evidenced in successful startups.

The dream is to create a successful startup inside the organization and rather than necessarily IPO it (though we know of where this has happened both successfully and unsuccessfully), build out from the startup and establish a new line of business. We have also seen examples of where intrapreneurship has been used to develop and extend the life of the organization's current products and services.

Ian has been working, since 2012, with his friend and fellow researcher Dee Ortner (Dee is a researcher and educator working in the areas of executive development and entrepreneurship) to explore the relationship between HR, entrepreneurs and intrapreneurs. This has included research into what makes entrepreneurs and intrapreneurs successful and what can go wrong. We will draw on this work for this section of the chapter.

During the research we found a great definition of what an entrepreneur is:

> An entrepreneur sees an opportunity which others do not fully recognise, to meet an unsatisfied demand or to radically improve the performance of an existing business. They have unquenchable self-belief that this opportunity can be made real through hard work, commitment and the adaptability to learn the lessons of the market along the way.
>
> They are not diverted or discouraged by scepticism from 'experts' or from those from whom they seek backing and support, but willing to weigh all advice and select that which will be helpful. They are prepared not just to work seriously hard but to back their judgment with personal investment at a level which will cause problems if they are wrong about the opportunity. They understand that achievements are the result of teamwork and knows how to choose the necessary blend of talents and inspire them with their vision.

(Chris Oakley OBE, Chairman of Web Design Company Chapter Eight; as reported in www.freshbusinessthinking.com, 2010)

Many of today's organizations are looking to develop this capacity internally both in their employees and as part of their management or operational mode. They believe, rightly or wrongly, that by encouraging employees to take risks, avoid the naysayers, work hard and be adaptable, the organization will reap the rewards of innovation and employees will learn and benefit from the process.

Organizations have always sought ways of increasing their innovation and continue to do so. The 1940s 'Skunkworks' are a good example of this. The idea was developed at Lockheeds Advanced Developments Projects Division to stimulate (and it successfully did) innovation in aircraft design. The concept involved taking a group of R&D engineers, allocating them access to resources, keeping them shielded from the bureaucracy of the mainstream organization and letting them do their thing! The idea was later championed by Tom Peters and Nancy Austin in their 1994 book *Passion for Excellence* and has been replicated to varying degrees of success in a number of organizations in all sectors. It has been criticized by many people and organization thinkers as making innovation the exclusive purview of the few, when they believe we should be finding ways of enabling all employees to innovate and discover their inner intrapreneur.

Organizations are seeking to develop intrapreneurial ways of working to:

- Increase innovation and creativity in the hope of developing new ideas, products and services or ideas that will enhance or refresh current products and services
- Challenge the status quo and have people break patterns of complacency and 'jobs worthiness'
- Unleash intrapreneurship, wake people up and get them to recommit to their jobs and the vision and goals of the organization. In other words, to avoid the organization becoming stale and having employees 'retired on the job'
- Take cost out of the organization, finding innovative ways of reducing the time and resources required for current products and services

Organizations tend to structure intrapreneurship in two ways, either in a special unit, or by launching groups. Special units are tasked with spreading innovation across the wider organization. This involves running innovation labs and ideation sessions and helping others learn how to create their own intrapreneurial space and unleash innovation. Launching groups aims to unleash intrapreneurship through the modern-day equivalent of skunk works, with a specific focus and shielded from the constraints of the wider organization. These groups share some of the similarities of project teams mentioned above but people are chosen to be members usually for their assumed sense of creativity and innovation as well as their knowledge of the issue in hand. Organizations that wish to have a more inclusive approach will use a crowdsourcing approach to identify and processes new ideas from a large number of people, in some cases extending beyond the organizational boundaries.

We have also seen companies attempt to raise their game with regard to intrapreneurship through acquisitions. The idea being that by purchasing a company that demonstrates a high level of intrepreneurialism they will be able to reap the rewards of this capability across their organization.

There are of course some very real problems with intrapreneurship. These mostly relate to organization culture and include:

- Most organizations develop a culture of risk aversion and find the risks inherent in intrapreneurship difficult to handle both practically and psychologically
- Keeping the organization's bureaucracy at bay more often than not proves difficult if not impossible. The corporate antibodies, as we like to call them, are always on hand and ready to destroy what they consider a foreign invader
- The strength of self-belief required and evidenced by intrapreneurs so essential to the success of the startup is often mistaken for arrogance and considered a bad thing within the organization. Organizations, particularly hierarchies, rely on a sense of sameness; people feeling part of the collective and not standing out. We have all heard of what is often described as 'Tall Poppy Syndrome'

- Organizations contain many expert functions and often rely on the bought-in functional expertise from world-class (and other-class) consultancies. It is harder for organizations to ignore what they are saying than it is for the startup
- Entrepreneurs have a massive amount of personal investment in their startup. This includes financially – in many cases their homes are on the line; reputationally – they have taken their big idea out into the world with no safety net and understand they may fail; emotionally – they may have spent many years thinking about their idea and it is not uncommon to hear entrepreneurs call it their 'baby'. It is almost if not impossible for an established organization to recreate these conditions with any authenticity. We have seen them try but not succeed
- The way in which teams of intrapreneurs are put together is more often than not based on personality rather than a true test of their intrapreneurial capability. Being part of the team is an exciting opportunity and we have seen people clamouring to be a part of it regardless of their true skill or level of capability. Starting with the wrong people is not a good place to start!
- In some circumstances we have seen organizations bring in an entrepreneur to stimulate intrapreneurship. Again this often does not work as ultimately the entrepreneur finds the corporate world too stifling and unresponsive. In turn after the initial honeymoon period the organization find the entrepreneur turned intrapreneur too maverick and troublesome. We know of cases were they have received a very healthy payoff to go away and used this to build a successful startup!

We will end this section with a story about a company trying to acquire intrapreneurial capacity and ways of working though merger and acquisition activities. A mid-sized company bought a startup that was establishing itself and just beginning to go global. The acquisition was driven by a desire to acquire the target's products and services, but more importantly its capacity for innovation. Of course this innovation capacity was based in the employees of whom there were about 5000 in five locations around the world.

The startup had a culture of openness and high levels of employee engagement. The acquiring company was excited about the possibilities this acquisition could deliver. There were many things they thought they could learn from it and replicate across the wider organization. It was ice cream that ended up causing problems! The acquisition had a policy of providing free ice cream and fizzy pop to employees during the summer months. This was not a policy that the acquirer had or supported for the rest of its employees. The corporate antibodies put a stop to it; the feeling being that if one part of the organization got ice cream then the whole organization would want it. It set a bad precedent.

What happened? Well the intrapreneurial capacity the acquiring organization had spent so much time and money courting and ultimately buying walked out the door! The acquirer ended up selling the organization off at a loss. You could argue this is simply an example of a poor acquisition integration strategy. We believe it is not just that. It is also about the difficulty mainstream organizations have in adapting themselves to allow for an intrapreneurial way of working.

Communality

The fourth way of working we have identified is that delivered by workplace communities. The remainder of this book will focus on the community way of working. Suffice it to say that in contrast to hierarchies, leadership in workplace communities is shared and all employees can freely become members regardless of their position, role or skill. In contrast to a project way of working, contributions happen when people feel inspired, not by a project deadline or the project manager telling them to do so. In contrast to entrepreneurism, everyone is required to act like an entrepreneur inside the organization. You will find a much fuller description in Chapter 3.

SUMMARY

One of the things that has surprised us in our research and working experience is that whilst there is a natural evolution from one way of working to the next, as organizations grow and mature, most of them contain all the ways of working described above, in some way or another. In many cases the organizations don't even know that these ways of working exist as employees have brought them into being by accident or by stealth.

This is more often than not in spite of management systems that allocate resources in ways developed to support purely hierarchical ways of working with occasional forays into program and project ways of working.

At the present time, the beginning of the twenty-first century and with the world coming out of the global financial crisis, we believe organizations must sincerely reflect on how their strategy and execution are best supported by the most relevant people processes and way of working.

Ways of working diagnostic tool

Way of working assessment – questionnaire

Instructions

The purpose of this simple tool is to help you to assess different ways of working that exist, and to help you determine if and when a particular way of working is most appropriate to what you are trying to accomplish (see Figure 2.1). Together with an understanding of the different ways of working, we hope the use of this tool will help you explore and consider alternatives to your default position. In particular, we hope this tool will help you give particular consideration to a workplace community. This is by no means a prescription on how you should organize the activities and tasks.

For each question (A–I), rank the four possible answers, giving a maximum score of 4 for the one that most reflects your situation, 3 for the next, 2 for the one after that and 1 to the answer that least reflects your situation.

Once you've ranked the answers to all questions you can transfer your score to the scoring sheet.

A. My Product/Service/contribution is...		Your ranking of the Answers Enter 4 for the highest, 1 for the lowest	
Q#1	An idea that I've been toying with for a while		
Q#2	Currently under development, backed by solid market research and a business plan		
Q#3	In development backed by solid Market research and a project plan with milestones and deadlines		
Q#4	Producing systematically the product/service based on an approved prototype		
B. My customers (or Potential customers) have...			
Q#5	Not been identified		
Q#6	Expressed interest in what I am doing		
Q#7	Helped my team develop the product specifications		
Q#8	Purchased and raved about the products/services and placed repeat orders		
C. The skills needed to achieve our task...			
Q#9	Are clear and within an expertise area		
Q#10	Are multiple and cannot reside in one person only		
Q#11	Are not easy to define at this stage		
Q#12	Are linked to risk management		
D. Rewards and recognition for my work is expected to be...			
Q#13	Based on pay scale and benefits to treat each employee equitably		
Q#14	Based on my competences and my contribution		
Q#15	Based on the risk I incur		
Q#16	Not monetary but linked to a recognition by my peers of my contribution		
E. The stakeholders of my organization expect...			
Q#17	Financial return in the short term		
Q#18	Nothing because they do not know about the initiative we are working on		
Q#19	Innovative product or services to be added to the portfolio		
Q#20	Financial return in the long run		

FIG 2.1 Way of working assessment – questionnaire

F. I prefer...	
Q#21	Having 'values' as the basis for managing company behaviors
Q#22	Having 'rules' as the basis for managing company behaviors
Q#23	Seeing evidence that our organization's values are implemented and alive
Q#24	Seeing evidence that behaviors go beyond and above the organization's values
G. The leadership of the organization, department or team resides...	
Q#25	In a clear line of command
Q#26	As distributed amongst its members with no hierarchy
Q#27	In the hands of a given member
Q#28	In the hands of a group of people
H. The funding for my work comes as...	
Q#29	A budget that is annually approved
Q#30	Linked to a fixed period
Q#31	A burn rate
Q#32	No budget allocated
I. The management systems governing my work...	
Q#33	Are centralized outside the team and is the same for every unit
Q#34	Are non-existent and there is no need to develop any
Q#35	Are used to monitor the progress of the task
Q#36	Are still to be scaled according to needs

FIG 2.1 Continued

Way of working assessment – scoring sheet

Instructions

Transfer your ranking score for each of the questions (Figure 2.2). The highest total score will suggest the best way of working for your activities.

Intrapreneurial	Program or Project	Hierarchical	Communality
Q# 2	Q# 3	Q# 4	Q# 1
Q# 5	Q# 7	Q# 8	Q# 6
Q# 12	Q# 10	Q# 9	Q# 11
Q# 15	Q# 14	Q# 13	Q# 16
Q# 20	Q# 19	Q# 17	Q# 18
Q# 23	Q# 21	Q# 22	Q# 24
Q# 27	Q# 28	Q# 25	Q# 26
Q# 31	Q# 30	Q# 29	Q# 32
Q# 36	Q# 35	Q# 33	Q# 34
Total	Total	Total	Total

FIG 2.2 Way of working assessment – scoring sheet

chapter 3

What Is a Community?

Introduction

In this chapter we will explore what we mean by a workplace community. We will explain what we see as its role and purpose and, perhaps even more excitingly, its potential for reshaping organization's life and the way we think about work. Moving work from the industrial to the internet or digital age.

Communities at work are a relatively new phenomenon. Their emergence has, to a large extent, been fuelled by technological advances in the tools and capabilities that allow us to connect and collaborate on a scale never before possible. These collaboration capabilities include many tools such as:

- Corporate email systems – which have existed for around 40 years and have become the default form of communication in most organizations since the 1990s.
- Bulletin boards and discussion forums – which have been around for over 30 years
- Corporate Intranets – which became prevalent in the early 2000s
- 'Web 2.0' capabilities such as blogs, wikis, micro-blogging, etc. that emerged around 2005

- Greater connectivity and networking in the workplace, new innovations in hardware and software and the possibilities of the cloud for the aggregation and interpretation of big data
- Web-based shared tools such as OneDrive, Dropbox etc.

In our lives outside of work, we may be very familiar with communities and may even be part of one; for example, face-to-face communities like book or film clubs and online communities about things that interest you or hobbies you might have. They are, however, much less common in the workplace and we are therefore not used to seeing or experiencing them in this context. Some of you reading this book may be wondering if they exist at all!

Our definition

Community is such an easy word for us to use and we all have our own perceptions and experiences of community both good and bad. When we use the word, we probably have ideas about physical, location-based communities in mind, as we typically live in them! However, in the context of the workplace what do we mean by the term community? There are many ways to describe organizations and organizational structures; business units, departments, cost centers, regions, functions, categories, silos, areas, etc., so what is a community in the context of the workplace?

Wikipedia defines community as having two distinct meanings:

(1) A usually small social unit of any size that shares common values, and
(2) In biology a group of interacting living organisms sharing a populated environment.
See: http://en.wikipedia.org/wiki/Community

Wikipedia is a great example of an online community where people come together to share knowledge and information and exercise their generosity to contribute to the development of understanding and knowledge. If you look at Wikipedia you may find this definition has changed. If so this will be a good demonstration of how communities develop and reshape ideas as they move forward. You may also not agree with the Wikipedia definition in which case join the community and start contributing!

Our general definition of a workplace community is:

> Where people come together and share intent, belief, resources, preferences, needs and risks, resulting in a common identity and sense of shared purpose.

The extent and intensity to which these conditions exist will drive the cohesiveness and the level of energy of the workplace community.

> A place, virtual or real, where people feel free to use their natural curiosity and inventiveness, coupled with a sense of generosity, to address issues and work on tasks that are important to them.

Communities are all around us

Communities are all around us and exist everywhere. They have existed since the dawn of time, since man and woman first shared things like places of safety, food and friendship with others for mutual benefit, safety and protection. Communities have provided the environment where humankind has evolved, developed and thrived over the millennia. We believe that communities are the oldest form of organization, of getting things done together and of people collaborating for a common purpose. All of us have belonged to many different communities both in and out of the workplace. We are sometimes members of a community without even knowing it! We take our membership for granted and spend little time thinking how it might be functioning.

Organizations are laced with workplace communities, often unseen, underutilized and at various stages of development. Regardless of the type of organization you work for, whether it be public, private or not for profit, there will be different types of workplace communities:

• Communities of practice, such as development groups for say Finance Managers

- Communities of interest, such as book or film clubs
- Functional communities like the finance community, the legal community, the HR community, the marketing community, the software engineering community, etc. coming together across organizational boundaries to share ideas
- Customer communities, formed to provide feedback and support to businesses.

The scale and size of these workplace communities will vary dramatically, from a handful of members to many hundreds, and we have even seen examples of workplace communities with many thousands of members.

The extent to which workplace communities are recognized and sponsored by the wider organization will vary tremendously. This is usually based upon the perceived value they create for the organization and the perceived level of disruption they cause. Some organizations may even feel threatened and challenged by them. Likewise, how active members of the workplace community will be depends upon the value they feel the workplace community adds to their work and life. In our experience, the majority of workplace communities will be invisible to most and their potential value to the organization not fully realized. Community members may gain a great deal, but if the connection between the workplace community and the wider organization is not very strong or not present at all, then the organization as a whole will gain very little. We have seen examples of where communities have been built 'bottom up' by individuals with a passion for a particular topic and only latterly gained the 'blessing' of the wider organization.

Even in the workplace

Workplace Communities can and do co-exist with the organizational structures we explored in Chapter 2. One of the interesting features and benefits of a workplace community is that it can and most often does cross-organizational boundaries and span departments. It can also breach the boundaries of the organization. We know of a number of examples where workplace communities include people who are not direct employees of the organization. We know of one community in an fast moving consumer goods company, that includes product developers from the local community as well as a network of school science teachers, whose classes get to 'play' with the companies molecules from a product development standpoint!

Just giving a group of people, an organization, a department or even a team the title 'workplace community' doesn't magically make it one! We know of a number of senior leaders who have heard about workplace communities and been tempted to do this. They simply announced that the organization was now a community, without the necessary conditions, approach or any other effort to make it real. Such announcements, from 'on high', are very likely to fail to engage people and will not unleash the benefits hoped for. They also run the risk of damaging the potential for true workplace community. You have to ask yourself why would people want to engage with something they have seen fail in the past? As much as you might like to, you cannot mandate people or force them to be members of a community.

We have seen this happen on a number of occasions. Senior leaders who become seduced by the latest organization fad, in this case workplace communities, tell people this is what they now are and wait to see what happens. Such communities tend to turn into little more than distribution lists. As you will learn through reading this book, initiating a workplace community is not quite as simple as saying, 'make it so!' It is not a difficult process but it does require certain conditions to be in place and systematic pre-planning of activities on behalf of those tasked with initiating the community.

We were once at a senior leader event for a global functional organization. The physical two-day event, held in a hotel conference facility, covered the usual array of business and strategy topics. It was well organized and very engaging. You could feel the high level of energy in the room as participants interacted with each other during the workshop sessions and especially during the coffee, lunch and networking breaks. Around lunchtime, on the second day, the leader enquired if there was a technology that participants at the event could use to continue the interactions and dialog. As it happened there was! In fact this same group of people all had access to a threaded discussion forum that had been used to support an earlier debate around reorganization. During the final session, the leader pronounced that we were now a global workplace community, and asked people to actively contribute to the online forum. The result was a general silence in the room. The leader became a little frustrated and asked for a show of hands from those who would commit to contributing to the online forum. Less than ten people raised their hands! The leader became more frustrated, explaining that he was serious about this and making it quite clear that he expected people to contribute. Again he asked for a show of hands. The number increased to around twenty. It is quite likely that those that raised their hands didn't know what they were committing to, or why, other than to the strong request of the senior leader of their organization. Following the event, there was some initial flurry of activity in the on-line discussion forum, but this diminished very quickly to zero.

To be a healthy functioning workplace community you need to build a common identity, a sense of purpose, a plausible promise, have tools that provide ways of interacting and an understanding of the bargain you are offering community members. It will be through the interaction and contribution of the community's members that you will ultimately establish and maintain the community and strengthen community members' sense of belonging and engagement.

Community members are keen to come together to meet an underlying need they share with others and want a domain where they can add value together as opposed to working alone. In doing so they create a domain that is outside of the confines and remit of the wider organization.

From what we have seen, people very often need to have the experience of a workplace community before being able to make their own contribution. In essence, communities don't exist because someone announces that they are a community, they exist when the members or potential members act and behave like a community and start experiencing the benefits. Oftentimes people's first experience of being part of a community is when they join a book or film club.

What needs to be in place?

Common identity – What is it that we have in common and are willing to give up our time to contribute towards? This is the object of our interaction and collaboration; something we have in common with others and can identify with.

With physical communities, location would typically offer us a common identity, as we all live in the same place, are associated with that location and share a common interests. In a workplace community the same condition is needed, but may be related to our professional focus, such as, production, finance, HR, software engineering, design, marketing, etc. It may relate to a product or a service that our organizations produce or deliver; it may relate to an initiative, program or project the organization has launched, or it may relate to an area not directly connected to the work of the organization; book reading, film viewing, management theory, ice hockey, football, zoology etc.

Sense of purpose – In addition to a common identity, there needs to be a sense of purpose. This is the reason for the existence of workplace communities. It is usually not sufficient for us to feel a common identity; we also have to want to do something about it. We feel the need to achieve something, driven by our personal sense of purpose. In a physical community, it may be a community effort to spring clean the local park or children's playground, or address what we perceive to be a road traffic hazard. In these examples, the general sense of purpose is to improve the environment in which we live, with a specific intent firstly to improve the condition of the park or playground and secondly to reduce the possibility of road traffic accidents.

In the workplace, this general sense of purpose also exists; for finance professionals it may be to develop processes to allow employees to manage expenditure and use finance metrics; or more specifically to improve the accuracy and timeliness of company reporting. For software engineers it may be to develop software engineering skills and capabilities, or a more specific intent, such as developing the next revision of a software-testing tool. So while as software engineers share a profession (software engineering), they need the sense of purpose to focus and channel their efforts in a workplace community.

Plausible promise – This means the 'what we are trying to do' in a community and together with the sense of purpose will provide answers to the questions:

- What is this all about?
- Why does this community exist?
- What attracts me to it?
- Why would I want to be part of it?
- What do we hope to accomplish by our coming together?
- Who else will be involved?

It is the plausible promise that creates the bond amongst community members. It is what links them together in common purpose.

The plausible promise needs to be believable, achievable, possible, realistic and most of all, plausible. It can be expressed as a call to action that ignites the community, or it may be subtler and less explicit and encourage people to come together to work it out for themselves. It is very important that the promise can realistically be achieved and does not sound to people like an invitation to come together to boil the ocean!

Here is a simple example of a call to action in a physical community that contains an explicit plausible promise; 'On a particular weekend, we as a community will meet up at a given time and will spring-clean the local park'. In our software engineering example of a workplace community it may be that we want to develop the new software test tool in the next 24 hours in a hackathon. For the finance community it may be that by month *ten* of this year we will have reduced the closing time from eight to six days, through our improved metrics and feedback processes.

A very good example of the above three elements is the Linux community that started over 20 years ago. In a single post to a news group

Linus Torvalds created a common interest, a sense of purpose and the plausible promise. It started off as an individual effort, but once Linus Torvalds shared this in a news group it was the start of a global community. Torvalds wrote:

Hello everybody out there using minix -

I'm doing a (free) operating system (just a hobby, won't be big and professional like gnu) for 386(486) AT clones. This has been brewing since April, and is starting to get ready. I'd like any feedback on things people like/dislike in minix, as my OS resembles it somewhat (same physical layout of the file-system (due to practical reasons) among other things).

I've currently ported bash (1.08) and gcc (1.40) and things seem to work. This implies that I'll get something practical within a few months, and I'd like to know what features most people would want. Any suggestions are welcome, but I won't promise I'll implement them :-)

Linus (torvalds@kruuna.helsinki.fi)

PS. Yes – it's free of any minix code, and it has a multi-threaded fs. It is NOT portable (uses 386 task switching etc), and it probably never will support anything other than AT-hard disks, as that's all I have :-(.

—Linus Torvalds

(Posted in comp.os.minix newsgroup, 'What would you like to see in minix? – Small poll for my new operating system', August 1991)

This simple posting, although full of technical terms, provides a common identity for 'those interested in these things'; provided a sense of purpose 'creating a free operating system'; and a plausible promise 'just a hobby, won't be big and professional, will only support AT hard disks!' It also provides a realistic timeframe, 'something practical in a few months'; and most importantly invites contribution 'I'd like to know what features most people would want'. Although giving no commitment to actually implement them!

The Linux community has obviously changed and developed significantly over the twenty years, and while it is no longer a workplace community, it does provide an excellent example of establishing the initial elements necessary for a workplace community. This is also a good example of one of the most important aspects of community in the workplace; authenticity. In this simple message you are left with a feeling that there is no hidden agenda. It will be the same with elements of a community in the workplace; they need to be authentic.

Tools – in physical, location-based communities this would be the physical 'tools' of the community, most usually a place where people meet and interact with each other. In a physical community, tools include flip charts, overhead projectors, white boards etc. In our digitally connected and social media-driven world, we have a huge variety of electronic and online tools that allow us to interact with people from all over the world almost instantaneously, in near real time and in ways that have never before been possible. We see millions, tens of millions of people coming together using the Internet to form thriving global communities. Yet within organizations, although they typically have the necessary tools and technology, all too often these tools and capabilities remain underutilized.

With the expectation of 'if we build it they will come', IT departments frequently launch tools and new technology with considerable fanfare enthusiasm and excitement. While there may be an initial spike in usage, or a core group of users (usually from IT) that use them on a regular basis, they rarely thrive in the longer term. Most large organizations are littered with unused or underused collaboration tools!

Many small organizations struggle to work out what tools are right for them and find it all too easy to be seduced by salespeople and consultants keen to sell them a new set of tools that promise a workplace revolution. For many organizations it is the fantasy that the right tools are a 'silver bullet' not just for cost savings, but also for increased engagement and a rise in productivity that drive purchasing decisions. Too often this leads to the wrong purchase choices, disappointment, cynicism and yet more organizational clutter. We will explore more about tools and provide you with help in making a choice as to what might work best for your community in Chapter 4.

In addition to the tools themselves, watch out for the tool owners! In our experience, people and individuals within an organization can become extremely protective over their tools. They will often have selected the tool, own it and see it as the best thing since sliced bread! It is not uncommon to hear the terms 'best of breed' or 'best in class' being used. corporate IT departments on the other hand, while having the mandate to provide the corporate infrastructure and deliver and support common tools, are driven by costs and the need for system integration. They are tasked with looking for the best overall fit. We have seen a lot of friction between tool owners and corporate IT. Tool owners want their technology to be recognized and used and corporate IT want only standardized technology inside the corporate firewall. At its worst, this can disrupt any attempts you make to initiate a workplace community and you may find yourself caught in the middle of a turf war. The search for the perfect tool and managing the politics of corporate IT can become a terrible distraction from the task in hand. We believe even an average tool, which is widely and actively used in the organization, is better than the latest and greatest tool that remains unused.

The Bargain – or 'what do I feel is in it for me?' This can be an explicit 'what is in it for me?', 'if I join this workplace community what do I get?' It can be about building my reputation, appearing on a leader board, or receiving some other form of recognition. However sometimes in workplace communities, the bargain is not as explicit as this.

The bargain is what drives members' contributions and can be very different for different people. Some people will feel good about sharing their knowledge, some will feel good about showing how much they know and how smart they are, some will feel good about helping and supporting others.

We have all heard the phrase in organizations 'knowledge is power!' If people hold this belief in your organization then you are likely to see people retaining information for their own purposes or even job security. They share information on a need-to-know basis or when they feel there is the chance of an even trade or an opportunity to raise their status. To shift from this culture to one of open sharing and transparency can be extremely difficult.

People are driven by how their activities and actions make them feel. In a workplace community the explicit bargain is: if I contribute my knowledge, I will expect (though there is no guarantee) that others will do the same. As a result, we will all learn and I, personally, will benefit from being a community member. Spending time focusing on the nature of the bargain for your workplace community will mean you are more likely to initiate one in which people feel free to share their knowledge and that their generosity will be rewarded by the generosity of others. In Chapter 8 we look in more detail at the nature and types of rewards that individuals as well as the wider organization can achieve through engaging with a workplace community.

One attribute of the bargain is the degree of competitiveness within the community: at one end of the spectrum is caring and sharing. Here community members generally feel good about giving, sharing and contributing for the greater good. These workplace communities can often be seen as support groups, helping people deal with difficult issues and difficult times. For example, managing a reorganization, company downsizing or rightsizing. At the center of the spectrum are collaborative and cordial workplace communities, where members give and receive. For example, workplace communities that focus on product or service development. Finally at the other end of the spectrum there are overtly competitive and even combative communities where there must be winners and losers. Online gaming communities are very good examples of the competitive and combative communities – the bargain here is very clear, and players know this; by competing you may win, but sometimes you will also lose. In competitive and combative communities the results are explicit – the winners are announced, top ten lists are published.

We cover more on the personal rewards of a workplace community in Chapter 8.

The management system

Organizations have management systems. These are the collective processes that control how the resources of an organization are allocated and used. The management system will include elements like strategy, budgeting, goals and objectives, reviews, audits and so on. The management system will enforce structure and practices for the organization and will enable the leadership of an organization to have reports and know the status of any actions.

Typically, management systems will follow a hierarchical model, strategy, goals and objectives are cascaded from the top to bottom, and status reports flow from bottom to top. It is unlikely that a management system will encompass the concept of a workplace community directly. However in the wider organization, the management system is the context, the environment in which a workplace community will exist. In many ways, workplace communities exist in spite of the management system. It is not that they subvert it but they seem to operate within and around it. You could argue they inhabit a different dimension.

Bringing it together

When you have a common identity, sense of purpose, plausible promise, the right tools and a bargain in place, you have all the ingredients and the basic elements for a workplace community. People will be drawn by the identity that they associate with; they will want to be part of it as they share the sense of purpose and be reassured by the plausible promise. Where the sense of purpose is strong enough, the tools are in place and the bargain felt, then workplace community members will contribute, even when it may not be in their best personal interest to do so. By this we mean that contributing to a workplace community may not be included in their personal tasks, objectives and targets and what their job descriptions say they are supposed to be doing. They are giving their discretionary effort.

Most organizations will have some form of performance management systems in place as part of their overall management system. They spend time setting goals and objectives and cascading these within the organizational structure (or silo!) to individual employees. The individual employee is held accountable for their contribution in meeting these pre-defined objectives.

We can remember interviewing a very active community member a few years ago; he was a software engineer, in his late twenties. We asked how much of his time he spent contributing to an open source software community. His very honest answer was that he spent as much time as he could, evenings, weekends and during the working day, when possible. He said that he believed in the purpose of the community and felt he was making a significant and meaningful contribution. He appreciated the interaction with and feedback from other community members. Unfortunately, when it came to his performance appraisal at the end of the year his line manager didn't see it the same way. The manager thought that he could and should have achieved more in his 'day job'. This was then reflected in his performance review and ultimately resulted in a reduced bonus payment. The irony in this particular case was that while the open source community was of little direct value to the line manager and the department he represented, it was of enormous strategic value to the company! They young software engineer told us that regardless of his manager's feedback he would continue to contribute to the community; his reputation depended on it. We believe his next job would most likely depend on it as well. He also asked if it was possible to work as a 'freelancer' within the organization that employed him, thereby not having to report to a line manager.

Different types of community found within the formal organization

We have found four types of community within the formal organization:

Unrecognized – Invisible to the organization and even sometimes to the members themselves. It is quite usual for groups of people to collaborate, share, and support each other within organizations. By doing so, they are acting in a community way often without realizing it.

The challenge with unrecognized communities is that they have not made a conscious choice to be a workplace community. Key contributors and members may be perfectly happy with the status quo and not see any added value in changing. They may not want the attention and expectations of the wider organization, or to become visible and open.

Bootlegged – This is a community that is visible informally to a circle of people 'in the know' it is typically a tight-knit and closed community. Membership is by invitation only. The challenges with a bootlegged community are that they have difficulty gaining resources beyond those that the members have access too, have limited influence and impact within the wider organization, are quite often hidden and fail to gain wider legitimacy. Bootlegged communities can be a very powerful lobby force.

Legitimized – These workplace communities are officially sanctioned as being valuable to the wider organization, and will receive support and resources as a result. The challenge for these communities is that they are under constant scrutiny; held accountable for their use of resources, effort and time which creates pressure in the short term. If this pressure is felt too early in the workplace community life cycle it can stunt or even prevent the further development of the community. This will lead to community members not wanting to take risks or put their heads above the parapet.

Institutionalized – These are workplace communities that are given official status and function within the wider organization. Typically it will have taken some time for the community to achieve this. However, once achieved it is assumes a 'business as usual' way of working. The challenge for institutionalized communities is that they will typically have a fixed definition and associated expectations. Given the status and expectations associated with this, it is likely that the community will be over-managed to ensure the expected outcomes. And lastly, once institutionalized, a community may well live beyond its usefulness, continuing to exist but unable to transform itself due to its fixed function and status. Institutionalized workplace communities more often than not turn into a mirror image of the wider organization.

How workplace communities differ from other ways of working

Communities combine hierarchy and fluidity

Communities are not just a collection of people with a common purpose; they are certainly not chaos. Structures and roles are needed. These will either emerge or can be established. Communities differ from formal organizations in terms of roles and structures in that they can change and develop over time far more quickly. Roles can be shared or shift as required and structures are only kept in place for as long as they are useful.

We will dedicate more time in Chapter 4 to exploring roles in more detail and providing you with outline role descriptions. Here we will introduce you to three categories of roles that are key to establishing your workplace community.

Initiators and leaders of the community

The initiators and leaders of a community play a key role in establishing the conditions that will enable a workplace community to take hold, grow and develop. We like to think of this as being like the role of a gardener. The gardener prepares the soil, plants the seed, waters the ground and removes any impediments to growth, such as weeds and rocks. They protect the early stages of development from threats, such a birds or other dangers. But the gardener is not the plant, nor is he or she the sun or rain that gives the plant life and nourishment. As with a plant it will take time for a workplace community to grow and develop. Expecting to harvest too early in the life of a workplace community may prevent it reaching its potential and can lead to stunted growth or even early death.

Leaders and initiators of workplace communities need to understand their role in relation to the community and its members. They need to be sensitive to the developmental stage the workplace community is at and, with this understanding, choose when to make an intervention and when not to. Good gardeners know how to make the right choice about what to grow where. They don't just grow plants for the sake of it. They choose which plants are needed whether they be vegetables or flowers. They don't want a glut or for everything to fruit or flower at once, so too with good community initiators and leaders.

One challenge that workplace initiators and leaders face is making sure that the community does not become all about them. We call this the 'queen bee' effect. The queen bee becomes the center of all activity, the focus of everyone's attention with community members buzzing around serving and trying to meet the needs and demands of the leader. Again we will deal with this in more detail in Chapter 6.

We suggest that a better approach for workplace community initiators and leaders is to be more like gardeners. That is, establish the conditions for the workplace community to flourish, ensure nourishment is possible and resources are available when required. In doing so, they will resist the temptation to put themselves at the center of the workplace community, to become the center of attention and to require all things pass by them and be blessed by them.

One of the most successful community leaders we worked with described his leadership role as being 'the mother' of the community. He would personally welcome new members, share the purpose and intent, and ensure resources were available when needed, but would refrain from being a key contributor. This was even though he had considerable content expertise. He would actively encourage and support community members, connect members with each other, but would not step in with his own thoughts and opinions unless explicitly asked to do so. He allowed the community the space to shape its own destiny, and did not dictate a pre-defined agenda. This hands off approach may well be counterintuitive to experienced leaders of organizations or project teams who are used to directing and being in charge.

Key contributors

Without contribution, a workplace community will be little more than a dormant mailing list. Contribution is critical. In any healthy workplace community there will be a group of people who will be key contributors to the community. Depending upon the nature of the workplace community, the number of key contributors will change and shift over time. When the topics and areas of activity shift, so too will the people who are making a key contribution; new key contributors will emerge as older ones move out of that role and into other roles.

Contribution is needed at all stages of workplace community development. We would argue that when the level of contribution starts to fall away the community has reached a transformational stage. It will then either re-focus and in doing to re-energize community members or it will close and die. Hopefully it will have been a positive experience and remain a good memory for all the former members.

Key contributors are particularly important in the early stages of a workplace community. It will be the contribution of these members and the interactions between them that other members and potential members will see and emulate. Key contributors act as role models with their contributions. Through contributing they allow other members to observe and experience the benefits of being a member of a workplace community and provide the encouragement to join in.

It is our experience that key contributors very often already exist within organizations. Typically they form private networks and tend to actively share information, thoughts and ideas and seek support within their private networks. Some, perhaps many, of these private networks have the potential to become workplace communities if the members are willing to exhibit exactly the same behavior in more open forums and more publicly within the organization. This openness and transparency will enable others to benefit from their sharing and interactions and also allow and enable others to join in and contribute.

The opening up of a private network can be a great kick-start for a workplace community initiative, although the shift from private conversations to public ones can be quite daunting for people. An additional challenge is that while subject matter experts may be comfortable with sharing ideas and exchanging views with a known group of people whom they consider to be peers or fellow subject matter experts, adding perceived novices, or large numbers of unknown participants may not be seen positively.

Community members

Members is the third category of role within the workplace community. Typically, this will be the large majority of the people involved. Members consume and disseminate the information shared within a workplace community, so play a vital role in this respect. In addition, they will provide occasional inputs. This can even be in the smallest way, perhaps a 'like' on a comment or by responding to a poll. Over time and as they become more familiar with the culture and spirit of the community they are likely to make more of a contribution. As the work of the community shifts to areas where they have more confidence and or greater knowledge and experience they may then move to becoming key contributors. Or they may simply become community elders; respected and influential members of the community.

Membership life cycle

Members will follow their own life cycle of membership. Initially they will be:

- **Visitors** – Often anonymous; people with a curiosity and a common sense of identity about the community, ready to take a look, to see what is happening, but not yet ready to sign-up.
- **Novices** – New members to the community who have registered and are now known as members ready to participate.
- **Regular members** – These regulars are comfortable participating in the community although their contribution level will vary.
- **Key Contributors** – From the regulars and/or key contributors leaders will start to emerge, people who will take on the responsibility of keeping the community running.
- **Elder** – Trusted long-term regulars, key contributors and leaders who have established and maintained their reputation over the life time of their membership.

It is common for community leaders to question the value of members who appear to be completely passive. We have more than once heard the request for these passive 'lurkers' to be removed from the community, since there is a perception that they add no value! Removing these passive members will of course prevent them from ever becoming active and moving through the stages of membership should they so choose to. We would advise against the removal of lurkers, they will learn and potentially share knowledge from the community and the have the potential to contribute in the future. They may also be making use of their experience of work place communities in other areas of the organization. The community may well have become a place of 'silent inspiration' for them and as such is making a major contribution to their life and work. Just because you don't see the value of their silent participation, doesn't mean there isn't any.

Do not expect every member of a community to contribute equally. Communities will have a predictable imbalance of contribution that will normally follow the 'power law distribution' (Figure 3.1). Simply put 80 percent of the contribution will come from 20 percent of the members.

Unlike hierarchical or project organizations where roles and responsibilities are pre-defined, and where outcomes are expected related to specific roles, communities can embrace a large number of participants whose contribution may be nothing more than a single idea, a tag, a like, a favorite. Unlike other forms of organization and ways of working, communities are able to tap into the 'long tail' – the 80 percent of members who contribute 20 percent. This ability to tap into and to

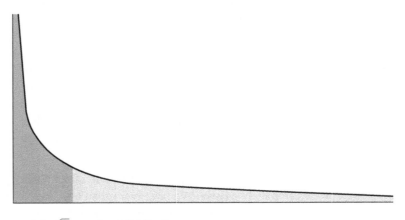

FIG 3.1   Power Law distribution curve

access the long tail enables a diversity of contribution and is one of the reasons why a community can be the source of great creativity and innovation. (Anderson, 2006).

Cultural diversity

In global workplace communities, do not underestimate the influence of the organizational culture; HQs versus subsidiary, global versus local, and national cultural norms. These will influence the behavior and contribution of members. While members sitting in the corporate HQ may feel quite comfortable discussing issues with the CEO and among themselves, it is quite another case for someone in a far off location to do and feel the same. National behaviors and cultural norms will be clearly seen in global workplace communities. Different cultures have different relationships to perceived power and as such, it is important to remember that just because someone isn't seen to actively contribute, doesn't mean that their participation is not of value.

A workplace community in Asia was asked to co-create a new policy. It was agreed that they would use a wiki to facilitate the co-creation. They agreed and indeed three months later the policy was published as had been requested. We interviewed them on how they had achieved the result. Instead of using the wiki to co-edit and co-create the document, they had only used the wiki at the end to copy/paste the final and approved version of the policy. They had worked exactly to their cultural norms, with one person creating the initial draft, submitting it via by email it to their manager for review, making necessary changes, and finally submitting it for approval. Only when their manager had approved the document did they feel they were able to share it in the wiki – and it was 'locked.' So even though there was the possibility for the workplace community to produce something in a new way, in this case they followed their behavioral and cultural norms.

Fluidity of roles

There are no fixed roles in a workplace community. Depending on the workplace community and the stage of development it is at, individuals will perform different roles and sometime multiple roles at different times, related to different topics. Roles can be given, or can emerge from within the community. When assigning roles to a workplace community it is important to spend sufficient time ensuring the person taking the role understands it in the context of a workplace community. They need to understand that leading a project or a program is very different from leading in a workplace community.

Community leadership

By its very nature community leadership is different from other forms of organization leadership. In traditional hierarchies, leadership and management responsibility is usually awarded and achieved through processes of recruitment, selection and talent management. The majority of people will transition into managerial or leadership roles as their career progresses – that is unless a close relative owns the firm – in which case their career may have a different and faster trajectory! One of the dilemmas we have encountered when talking to leaders and manages is how much they miss being a practitioner. The management or leadership role is not all that they had expected. They miss being a lawyer, accountant, software developer etc. and the demands of the leadership role is driving out the parts of the job they enjoyed the most.

Leadership and management can be incredibly fulfilling roles. However, they often involve people moving out of their comfort zones, moving away from holding expert power and having to adopt a different set of behaviors to get things done. Too often people fall into stereotypes as to how they think leaders and managers should behave and deliver. This can include at its extreme high levels of game playing and even bullying.

In a workplace community leadership is handled differently. The community provides a wonderful opportunity for people to experiment with their leadership style and approach. Leadership tends to be taken on by community members around issues that are important to them and once those issues have been addressed or resolved those who held the reins for that aspect of the community's work can let go and allow others to take on the leadership role. Leadership is free flowing and community members recognize at an intuitive level that they do not need to lead on everything. Leadership becomes a servant to the work of the workplace community; doing what needs to be done to allow the community to function and fulfill its scope and purpose. It is more of a facilitating function.

The idea that leadership is shared and a shifting function in a community can often be experienced as a scary one! People we have talked to about how leadership differs imagine and expect that the workplace community will descend into chaos and anarchy. This has not been our experience. We believe that if you set up your workplace community as we suggest then you will find that leadership becomes a function that is exercised with appropriate gravity, care and thought. It just looks different.

The workplace community can be a wonderful place for individuals to test out their leadership capabilities. They may not have a formal leadership or management role within the wider organization, but given their specialist knowledge and experience and its relevance to the activities of the community at that time, they may choose, or as we have seen, feel compelled by something within them, to take on a leadership role. This provides them with the opportunity for real-time development and to get feedback on how they have been experienced as leaders. It also provides the wider organization with the opportunity to talent spot and enrich succession planning.

The benefits of community

There are many ways in which a community will be of benefit to the organization, as well as to its members. Value will be created in both the short and the long term. In general, short-term value to the organization will be related to improving business outcomes; in the long term the value will be related to developing organizational capabilities and enhancing employee engagement.

For the individual, the benefits in the short term will generally be related to improving their experience of work, and in the longer term fostering their professional development.

It should be noted that the benefits of a workplace community, even the short-term benefits, will not be achieved until the community has reached a certain level of maturity, this will take time and effort, but once achieved will be more than worth the investment.

We suggest you tailor the list below to fit your organization and then use this to engage with stakeholders about the ideas of workplace communities. We will explore more about engaging stakeholders in Chapter 4.

Individual benefits of a workplace community

Short term

- Sense of belonging
- Access to expertise and knowledge
- Better able to contribute to the team and the organization as a whole
- Builds confidence in one's approach to problems
- Help and support with challenges
- Fun of being with colleagues
- More meaningful participation
- Increased understanding of the organization
- Greater engagement

Long term

- Forum for expanding skills and expertise
- Network for keeping abreast of a field
- Enhanced professional reputation
- Increased marketability and employability
- Strengthened sense of professional identity
- A place to test yourself and try on different identities, ways of being and working
- A place to try out ideas
- A chance to see the organization 'in the round' through meeting people you would never normally encounter
- A development opportunity

Organizational benefits of a workplace community

Short term

- Arena for problem solving
- Quick answers to questions
- Reduce time and costs e.g. development time
- Improved quality of decisions through broader contribution
- More perspectives
- Increased engagement
- Resources for implementing strategies
- Strengthened quality assurance
- Ability to take risks with backing of community
- New entrants to the organization get to contribute quicker

Long term

- Ability to execute a strategic plan through broader access to ideas and solutions
- Greater client centricity, with clients sometimes being invited to join workplace communities
- Increased retention of talent
- Capacity for knowledge development projects
- Forum for benchmarking against rest of industry
- Knowledge-based alliances
- Emergence of unplanned capabilities
- Capacity to develop new strategic options
- Ability to foresee technological developments
- Ability to take advantage of emerging market opportunities
- The discovery of new talent
- Increased potential for organization development
- Finding out something new as well as confirming what you already knew
- A force for organization change
- A license to explore critical organization issues – if the community has 'diagnosed' an issue this can confirm what you knew but have not had support to work on.

Positives and negatives of the workplace community

Workplace communities can be seen as a threat to other forms of organization. Leaders and managers of the wider organization may fear that 'their resources' will be spending valuable time contributing to a community effort and not using this time for the direct benefit of their business unit or team. In our opinion this is a short-termist approach in today's knowledge-driven economy. We feel that good leaders and managers will appreciate that it is part of their role and their responsibility to contribute to the development of the whole organization, while of course managing their particular part of it. This is not always the case and we will address this issue and other forms of resistance in Chapter 4.

Workplace communities can promote a safe, high-trust environment. The strength of the relationships formed provides a climate where people can openly share what they think, share their ideas and take risks; knowing that they are doing so with the support of the community.

Reputations will be formed within the community through individuals' contributions and the visibility of these. Very often opinion leaders emerge from within the community. This can enable the location and access to expertise. If it were not for the workplace community, these experts would remain in likelihood unknown!

Imagine having a specific business challenge or problem that you have discussed with your manager and close colleagues but so far without finding a solution. They might suggest other people whom they think may be able to provide you with help and support. You contact these people but unfortunately this does not result in a solution. They may in turn refer you to others and so on. You end up having spent considerable time and energy desperately trying to connect with a person or persons who can help you solve your problem, using your and other people's networks.

Now imagine that your organization has a workplace community in some way related to the subject of your challenge or problem. You know that this community exists, but have not been an active member. Having asked your immediate colleagues for help, but without success, you turn to this community. It may well be that when searching the community database; you find that the challenge you face has already been a topic within the community. You discover that there has been a thorough exploration and multiple solutions documented that you can immediately apply. Or perhaps you are the first to face this challenge, and so simply pose the question to the community, not really knowing who, if anyone, will respond. Now imagine that within a very short time (perhaps mere minutes) someone you have never met, never heard of before, responds and provides you with the solution to your challenge. When you experience this generosity, this sharing of knowledge from a complete stranger, you are experiencing the power of a workplace community. This type of interaction is very common within flourishing and healthy workplace communities.

So when is a workplace community right for you?

As a general guideline, a workplace community will be appropriate when you want to accomplish one or more of the following (also see Chapter 4):

- Share ideas
- Explore new areas
- Have discussions and get diverse point of views
- Connect people from different parts of the organization
- Gain comments and feedback from a wide audience
- Find solutions and good and best practices
- Invite contributions
- Leverage social learning
- Drive engagement

The development and use of a community will be less appropriate when you wish to accomplish one or more of the following:

- Force contribution to a certain task or topic – people will be active in what interests them and not what is necessarily important to you
- Require immediate contribution and deliverables

- Manage to a tight deadline
- Not build on or develop collective intelligence
- Deal with sensitive and/or bureaucratic issues or projects (e.g. outsourcing)
- Or, when you have no time or desire to cultivate the community.

Below is a list of critical success factors for a workplace community. We suggest that you use this as a checklist, and to identify actions to share with your stakeholders.

Table 3.1   Community critical success factors

Critical success factors		
Issue		Actions
Focus on topics important to the business and interesting to community members • People can see the value of the community • Help to build personal relationships among community members		
Coordination of the community exists with dedicated people or well-respected community members • Hosting and leading a community is seen as a career development path • Develop an active passionate core group		
Make sure the members have time, space and encouragement to participate • Trust in collective intelligence • Community is seen as a credible way of working • Recognition structures – voluntary contribution is recognized/awarded		
Create Forums for thinking together as well as systems for sharing information • Technology support is available (e.g. wiki tools) • People are able to and like to use the tools • Necessary training can be provided • Make it easy to contribute and access the community's knowledge and practices		
Regular communications or facilitation events • Working practices are defined • Create real dialogue about cutting-edge issues		

4

Getting Started – Elements of Effective Community

Introduction

In this chapter we will explore and share the practical things you need to do if you have decided that a community way of working is right for you. In Chapter 2 we introduced you to the 'ways of working questionnaire' and we hope this will have helped you to make the right decision. We also suggest that you share this book with your friends and colleagues and talk through your ideas with them.

The issue you want to address

By now you should have an issue or some topics that you think a community way of working might help you address. The issue or topics needs to be something that is important to you and that you do not believe you are able to sort out or resolve on your own.

SCENARIO PART 1

To make this chapter as practical as we can, we have developed a case study. This is based on our experience but changed enough so as not to break any confidentiality agreements we have in place with our clients. As you will have seen for most of the book we have been 'organization agnostic' that is we believe that workplace communities are applicable to any organization, regardless of its main focus or type.

Imagine you are part of a team of software architects. Your actual role or level of seniority does not matter. The team is finding it increasingly difficult to recruit and retain staff in all roles. As a team you have explored all the obvious issues, such as pay and benefits, team culture and ways of working. All of this seems to be OK and comparable with other organizations, but you still have this problem. This issue is increasingly impacting on the ability of the team to produce results and meet its tasks and targets. As you have tried all the traditional ways of addressing the issue you are thinking that a workplace community may be worth a try. Here are a few more details about the team and the wider organization: team size – 150 of which 100 are dedicated software engineers and 50 are in leadership, managerial, coordination and support roles. The organization has been around for 15 years and employs 4,000 people. These people are distributed around the world mostly based in 6 major locations.

We will come back to this scenario as we work through the process of getting started, so this was just an introduction.

Community scope, purpose and name

Before you launch your ideas on the organization you need to spend time defining the theme and scope of your workplace community. By theme we mean the broad area of inquiry and by scope, what you want to focus on within this broad area. Think carefully about what you want to use your community for. However also be aware that as you initiate the community others may shift your thinking and the theme, scope and purpose may change. This can be both a good and a bad thing. Good in that people may well know things that you did not have any idea of when you were thinking through the process. This will add richness to the community and opens up the possibility of something new emerging. It can be bad, in that the community may get 'hijacked' and start working on things that are nothing to do with the issue in hand. We will deal with this hijacking issue in Chapter 6.

Your theme and scope need to be clear and concise so that you can share it easily with potential community members, as well as other key stakeholders. This is not about certainty but about having as much clarity as you can. You need to be confident enough to share those areas where you lack clarity and to seek help from others. This is often very difficult for people as organizations encourage us to work within a broad scope of certainty and the more senior we are the more certain, clear and knowing we are supposed to be.

Launching a community without clear boundaries, certainty of outcomes and fixed roles can be a real challenge in a climate where certainty is expected, even demanded. However it is precisely these attributes that will help to make your community successful. It will provide all community members with the opportunity of contributing more widely and working outside the given norms of the organization, in different ways, that lead to the possibility of something new, different and exciting emerging.

If at the initiation stage you offer too much or false clarity or have set the boundaries and expectations too tightly, you will find that people will be reluctant to engage and join. On the other hand, without a shared sense of purpose and scope or a high-level theme, you will struggle to get people to join at all. They won't want to commit to something that is so open ended they have no idea what they bring to the community, what are they contributing to or what might be expected of them.

It is also worth pointing out here that not all communities are set up to solve problems or address issues. We know of some that have been set up to enhance learning and sharing across the organization and have been very successful in doing this. Very often these workplace communities transition into communities of practice or communities of interest.

In our scenario the theme would be recruitment and retention and your scope software engineers.

Plausible promise and igniting questions

Lynda Gratton, in her work on 'hot spots' (Hotspots, Gratton, L., 2007) uses the idea of 'igniting questions' to describe what is needed for people to come together and form a high-performing team. An igniting question is something that excites people and makes them want to contribute. In Chapter 3 we explored the idea of 'plausible promise' as something the workplace community needs to have to engage with people and encourage them to join. When planning to initiate a work place community we suggest you think about and explore with others, not just the theme, scope and purpose but also what would ignite and excite people and make them want to join. You should test this with people who have no previous knowledge of what you are planning and assess their response. Also think through the plausible promise you are offering them and just how realistic this is.

You need to have these elements aligned and expressed in such a way that they appeal to the right people and these people can share them with others who may also be able to contribute something to the work of the community. Your community will grow by both your own efforts but also importantly, and more often, through the networks of others.

You need to be clear on how you will deliver on your plausible promise. If you promise people something and are not able to deliver this then you will soon find that your workplace community dies, and along with it your reputation!

Naming your community

Thinking up an attractive name for your community is important. It needs to be something interesting and engaging, such that when people hear it, they want to know more and feel compelled to explore and find out. It is how people are likely to first find out about your community so it needs to be self explanatory and to catch their interest.

In our scenario the igniting question' could be something along the lines of:

'Why do people not want to join our team and why do you stay?'

The plausible promise could be along the lines of 'By exploring what is going on and why people don't want to join, we will be making the team a better place for all of us to do exciting and interesting work and help build the sustainability of the organization as well as develop ourselves.'

The name of the community could be something along the lines of 'software engineering – why do you stay?'

A quick audit

At this stage it is also worth checking to see if any other groups, task forces, teams or individuals are working on this issue. These can be either formal or informal groups. If there are others already working on the issue, it is worth exploring with them how successful they have been, how they have been working on the issues, who else is involved and what governance structure they have in place. If you do find other groups working on the issue, this does not mean that your workplace community does not have relevance, or is not the right approach. By doing this kind of quick audit you may just have found your first community members or even a ready made group of key contributors!

Through your audit, you find that corporate HR are currently in the process of developing a new employee value proposition for software engineers. They are aware of the attrition rates, recognize there is a problem and have been asked to address it. The CEO is also very keen that something happens soon as they can see the negative impact this is having on the business. Your initial reaction may be to give up on the idea of a workplace community, thinking that HR will now take charge and sort this issue out. However, we would encourage you to not give up yet! It is worth starting a discussion with HR about community ways of working, sharing with them the ideas in Chapters 3 and 5 and inviting them to get involved. This may be a difficult discussion to have. HR may question your legitimacy for wanting to get involved and feel they have sole ownership and responsibility and may well want to control and coordinate any actions. However if you have crafted a powerful igniting question and an inclusive, plausible promise then it should be easier to get them engaged. Having people interested in the idea and willing to share the burden could be very attractive to them. It is also important to be clear how the workplace community will be receptive to engagement from them and to demonstrate your own commitment to the issue. By doing so you will be modeling the kind of sharing and generosity that is at the heart of workplace community ways of working.

If HR is still 'twitchy' about this approach, you may want to suggest to them that they read this book! Or you could offer to run a short workshop for them on workplace community ways of working. It may also be possible to have them see this as an experiment and one that will help them with their role. In no way are you usurping or undermining their professional role and position in the organization. The experiment would also help them understand if workplace community ways of working might be something that could have a wider application in the organization and help them address other organization issues in a dynamic, inclusive and exciting way.

Getting agreement – managing stakeholders

Prior to initiation it is worth doing a quick stakeholder analysis to iden-tify the key people and groups in the organization who have, or feel they have, a legitimate interest in the establishment of the workplace community and the theme it will be working on. These people have the ability to offer their support and sponsorship or to say no to what you are planning to do. It is best to engage with them before you initiate as you are more likely to have a smoother ride as you get going. This is not always about seeking permission. It is more about building alignment to the idea and getting people on board. It is also about confirming that the issue you and the community will be working on is important to the organization and worth the effort.

We suggest you use the template below to help you identify your key stakeholders and what actions are needed to get them on board (Table 4.1).

It is important at this stage to understand the potential impact that the initiation and launch of the community is likely to have on others in the workplace. By engaging with stakeholders you can surface concerns and questions and address these up front. You can also start to build commitment to a workplace community way of working and at the same time you may find your first community members.

Table 4.1   Stakeholder engagement plan

Stakeholder engagement			
Stakeholder	Support required	Action needed	Who/When

Surfacing resistance

So you now have sorted out your scope and theme, and you have a name for your community. You have done a simple stakeholder analysis and identified the key players who you need to have on board. Now it is time to start engaging with them.

When you launch a workplace community, as with any new organization initiative, it is always best to know what kind of resistance and objections you are likely to experience. What you are likely to uncover, during discussions with your stakeholders, are most likely to be conscious and unconscious concerns they have about the organization as well as the idea of workplace community ways of working. Surfacing these will allow you to address them directly rather than having to deal with things that are constantly bubbling under the surface. If you are pre-warned you can plan how to address these concerns and get people onside.

Planning for stakeholders' meetings

Before a stakeholders' meeting it is vital that you do your homework. There are two areas we suggest you focus on as you plan your stakeholders' meetings.

Firstly be clear on the issue you feel needs to be addressed and why it is of importance to the organization as a whole. Think through its impact on current and future business strategy and the organization's aims, objectives, tasks and targets. You will also need to be clear on how it connects to the people you will be inviting to join your workplace community. If you can connect the issue to costs and not just benefits, then all the better.

The best way of doing this is to develop an elevator speech. That is a very short presentation that encapsulates your idea in about 90 seconds. If you go into your stakeholder meetings with a rambling long-winded speech you are likely to have lost your audience in the first five minutes. You need to be clear and concise. It may help to have a couple of slides, which outline the issue and its impact on the business. However you will know the style of your stakeholders and what works best with them in terms of presentations.

It may help you in terms of your presentation to think of the Organization Development (OD) metaphor of 'pain versus remedy'. What is the pain the organization is feeling, or is likely to start feeling by not addressing the issue and how would a workplace community approach be the remedy for this pain? Another classic OD approach would be to show how by not addressing the issue, the organization will be missing out on an opportunity. Be clear on how you will keep your stakeholder connected to the community whether or not they become a member. If you have specific things you need for them to do then now is the time to ask.

Secondly, be clear on what you mean by a workplace community, why you have chosen this particular way of addressing the issue and why you think it will work. At this stage in the discussion it would be good to share with them what else has been tried and how it has not worked, and the impact this has had on the wider organization and those specifically affected by the issue. It is also a good idea to share with them why you think the conditions are now right for this new approach and how it will work. You might choose to develop your own tailored scenario based on the one in this book, which you can share as an example of how things might work.

Having read this book you should be able to marshal your arguments! Be very clear on what a workplace community can do and what it cannot do and what the organization can expect. Be realistic and down to earth. If you oversell the idea then you will have problems later on managing overinflated expectations. You will also need to show how the workplace community will not be disruptive to production but simply be an extension of community members' day-to-day activities. You can also share with them ideas about employee engagement and tapping into people's discretionary time.

Have an outline plan to show how you intend to go about initiating and managing the community. We have included a draft plan in this chapter. Be clear on the roles the workplace community will need and the technology you will be using.

If you work through the above it will help you to have a productive dialogue and manage any concerns your stakeholders may have. However it is not at all unlikely that your conversation will surface questions you have not thought of and you are also likely to identify areas of resistance and challenge.

Resistance and challenge

In our experience, most of the challenges and expressions of resistance you face will fall into the following categories. With stakeholders perceiving your workplace community as:

- Challenging the **status quo** of the organization and potentially usurping the rights of managers and leaders to set the agenda, make decisions and generally lead and manage
- A **distraction** from the 'real' work of the organization, which is best done in a predictable and hierarchical way. Being controlled and managed
- Taking people's eyes off of **current reality** and being too much about the future, which is best left to take care of itself or by the highly paid help!
- Potentially unleashing **anarchy** in the organization. People might start to share things that are considered 'off topic', breaking confidences and generally disrupting the normal running of the organization
- Possibly encouraging fights to break out and the workplace community becoming a forum for people to air their **disgruntlement** with the organization as a whole. As such it will kill engagement and create misery
- In some way people may have a **vested interest** in things not changing and any potential for change threatens this

Here are some examples of how you can address the challenges described above:

- **Challenge the status quo** – you will need to reassure those concerned about this, that this is not your intention at all. Take them through what you have already learnt about workplace communities, how they operate and how they are managed. In particular you will need to show them how the community keeps connected with the wider organization and the benefits that working in this way can bring to the organization as a whole.

- **Distraction** – you will need to explain to them how the suggested community is connected to the overall strategy of the organization and how it will add value. You are simply suggesting a new way of working on issues of concern and not challenging the overall mission, vision, strategy etc. of the organization.

- **Day-to-day versus future orientation** – show them how the workplace community will be working on issues that are negatively impacting on the success of the organization today. Yes, there is likely to be discussion and exploration of the future, but at the same time the focus is on doing something to make things better today!

- **Anarchy** – even though in a community leadership is shared you will need to explain how people can self manage and the way in which contribution works. The workplace community will be an opportunity to unleash generosity as opposed to anarchy.

- **A forum for disgruntlement** – it is likely that members of the community will talk about issues that concern them and may even moan and groan a bit! However in our experience two things usually happen to stop this becoming all-consuming. Firstly, people get bored with moaning and also with listening to it; they either challenge themselves or get challenged by others to move on. Secondly, if you look closely at what they are moaning about, you may find some interesting things that can be very useful for the wider organization to address.

- **Vested interest** – this is a much more difficult one to address in any change situation. You will need to find a way in which stakeholders feel they have a choice about what to do with the outputs and outcomes from the work of your community and how they can feel connected as the process moves forward. If the issue is really acute then you may need to find others who support you and who can override this concern.

In summary it is also worth stressing that the workplace community you are proposing can also be a useful place for critical stakeholders to communicate how they are addressing issues in the organization. It will provide them with the opportunity to learn more about what is going on and potentially to get great ideas about how to lead and manage.

Tools and technology

Tools and technology are critical to the success of your community and at the same time they can also be a red herring! Workplace community initiators and members can become so obsessed with finding the perfect tool(s) that they forget to spend enough time on scope, purpose and theme, let alone on the plausible promise and igniting questions! This can become a major distraction from getting going and the noise of the technology and tools debate can drown out the issues the workplace community is being set up to address and work on. Tools need to be fit for purpose and are not the be all and end all of the community.

Even if your workplace community meets face to face you will still need ways of capturing the work of the community and managing its outcomes. Some form of knowledge management system is required. If, as is more likely, your community is a virtual one, then the tools are the way in which community members will connect and work together.

It is worth exploring what tools your organization already has and how they might fit the bill. You will find it easier to get traction for experimenting with a workplace community if you can use existing well-known and functioning tools and technology, rather than requiring expenditure on the part of the organization for something new. A new tool will come with a learning curve and again can be a distraction.

Where the appropriate tools and technology do not already exist in the organization, we have known of cases where workplace communities have been developed around externally available social media platforms like Facebook, LinkedIn and Google Circles+, utilizing the 'closed groups' these platforms offer. In addition to the popular social media platforms there are also a large number of internet community platforms available, typically offered as cloud-based services. Example of these are Ning, www.ning.com, and Socious, www.socious.com. (An internet search for 'online community platforms' will reveal many more). Some of these cloud-based services will require payment in the form of a monthly fee, others are offered free and may come with embedded advertising or other distractions. It is popular to offer a trial period for free, and then once you are hooked, for providers to charge either for continued use or to unlock some of the more advanced features and the most desirable functionality.

A lot of organizations however are not comfortable with the use of external tools and platforms that are not behind the company firewall, especially if anything that is considered confidential or sensitive is to be shared or discussed. So this will need careful exploration and agreement with key stakeholders before you proceed. You will not want to be changing the tools and technology once your community is flourishing. If not managed well this can be a major disruption and cause significant damage, especially if the move to any new tool or platform does not migrate the existing content and retain the context in which it was originally created.

The tools need to be able to support the types of interaction that you expect to have between your community members, typically these include (note this is not an exhaustive list):

- User administration and appropriate security
- A user profile, including a photo
- Ability to connect with and 'follow' people
- Allow for near real-time interactions
- Enable threads of conversations on different topics or subjects
- Enable sharing of documents and maintain versions controls
- Be searchable
- Archive information
- Allow for polling
- Have metrics and analytics built in
- Allow for co-creation as in a wiki
- Allow for feedback and recognition (likes, ratings, comments)

- Login and authentication (single sign-on is recommended, people don't remember additional passwords)'
- Ability to broadcast messages to members
- Ability to notify members of activity and updates

We are not going to prescribe specific tools; however here is a list of general criteria we suggest you use to help you make a choice. Your tools need to be:

- **Easy to use/Intuitive** – if people struggle to understand where to find the tool, how to login (which credentials to use), or how to use the tool, then this will become off-putting, frustrating and will inhibit and may stop them from contributing. They should require minimal training and be extremely intuitive. A general rule is that you lose 50 percent of your users for every mouse click they need to make!
- **Reliable** – it goes without saying that if your tools keep breaking down then people will become frustrated and leave. Equally if people lose things or cannot search, then you may find community members get frustrated, have to keep repeating things and will finally give up. If the tools are frequently unavailable people will not come back.
- **Accessible** – people may well want to engage in community activities outside of normal office hours and so having them be accessible from outside the corporate firewall and on multiple platforms as well as mobile devices will help usage. Obviously if you want members from outside your organization to participate, the tool will need to be accessible outside the firewall.
- **Scalable** – the tool will need to support the volumes of users that you are expecting to participate (concurrently or otherwise) without any degradation in performance. It will also be important for the tool to be able to accommodate all the content that the community creates over its entire lifetime. Additional capacity may be available for additional costs from cloud-based services.
- **Supported –** for any tool or platform you need to understand where you will receive support, what are the service levels offered and at what cost. Support needs can range from an individual user having access problems, through to the whole platform being unavailable to the whole community for an extended period of time!

Workplace community roles

In Chapter 3 we explored a couple of the primary roles you need. In this section we will look in more detail at the roles we believe are required to ensure your workplace community functions and operates successfully. Some of these roles, we believe, are absolutely necessary for the success of your community. Others are more of a nice to have. Some will need to be directly part of the workplace community and others need to be on hand to offer advice and support as needed. As a workplace community develops these roles may be assigned to community members, or in other cases will emerge from within the community, based on activity and contribution.

What we have found in our work is that although you may try to recruit and appoint people to these roles, that is you ask people to take on the roles, as the community moves from potential to coalescing then the roles start to emerge with people taking them on as they appear to be needed. As this happens community members may need support and coaching to fulfill them.

Unlike in the wider organization, roles in a workplace community tend not to be fixed, but are much more fluid. People take on a role when working on a topic they are interested in or feel they have something valuable to contribute. Once this work has come to a conclusion or the energy of the community has moved away from it, then roles are likely to shift and change. This is one of the beauties of workplace community ways of working, all members have the opportunity of experiencing what it is like to take a leadership role, be a facilitator or be a key contributor. They may also choose to experience being a lurker and simply watch what is happening. In large diverse workplace communities it may well be that a single person is performing many roles concurrently, leading, facilitating an area of interest, contributing to certain topics, and observing and lurking in other areas of the community.

Workplace communities provide employees with wonderful development opportunities that are often not available to them in the wider organization, because of position, status and role. However this fluidity of roles needs to be encouraged. Community members need to be comfortable in taking up a role as well as putting it down and letting others take over at the appropriate time. This can be particularly difficult for people who are used to very fixed roles in the wider organization. If they have a well-established and recognized leadership role then simply being a community member can be difficult for them. Especially if other community members challenge them about their behavior and in particular about what may be experienced as the inappropriate exercise of authority. However this can be a superb learning experience for them, if a little painful! Connecting them with how the wider organization experiences their exercise of leadership and in the longer-term help them refine and develop their practice. How people take on and succeed or fail in different roles, is also a great way of spotting potential talent that exists within the organization but may have not yet have been recognized.

Roles within a community are more negotiable than they are in the wider organization. That is, they do not need to be designated and fixed in the same ways, as they need to be in a hierarchy, or project, with job descriptions and fixed tasks and targets. They are emergent and people need to evidence the skills required as they go along and as the role is required.

Sponsor(s) – we believe these are nice to have but not essential at the initiation stage. By that we mean that if you have a sponsor then it makes things easier. We know of a number of examples in which a workplace community has been initiated and developed sponsorship only after it had been running for a while and people became interested and excited by what they saw happening. In our experience a successful workplace community, one that is recognized as being of interest and adding value to the organization, will naturally attract potential sponsors. People will want to be associated with success stories.

In classical OD and change management the sponsor's role is seen as vital in legitimizing the work being undertaken. A lot of programmatic change focuses on initially working hard to get sponsors aligned and on board. Many change initiatives are seen to fail as a result of a 'disappearing sponsor'; a sponsor, who drifts away from the initiative, loses interest or becomes part of the problem!

If you have a high level sponsor then it can be easier to attract community members and also garner resources to help support the work of your community. They may also be able to draw attention to the work of the community within the wider organization and help you implement the outputs. However if you don't initially have a sponsor do not worry too much.

Initiator – in essence this is likely to be you! The workplace community needs someone or a small group of people who will do the initial groundwork and planning. Things like setting the context, developing the theme and scope and having enabling conversations with key stakeholders and ultimately launching the community.

One of the challenges you are likely to face is balancing being a member of the community with having responsibility for ensuring the community stays connected to the wider organization and does not get lost and mired in the mud! As the community moves towards maturity this role will become shared and distributed amongst other community members who will help you do the heavy lifting.

Facilitators – again we would argue, that this is not a fixed role but one that should be shared and distributed. However during the coalescing stage you may need to identify people who will take on this role for you. As the workplace community moves towards maturity then, in a healthy community, community members will become self-facilitating and take on this role as needed.

The role of a workplace community facilitator is very similar to that of a facilitator in the wider organization. This includes, acting as a moderator, helping community members and groups that form within the community to unpick what they are doing and draw things to a conclusion. They may also need to challenge behavior that they feel is getting in the way of community activities. Facilitators may also take an active role in the rituals that develop in the community. These can include, creative processes, knowledge gathering and sharing and hosting events and activities.

Key contributors – these are people who have detailed knowledge of the issues the workplace community is working on. You can think of them as being subject matter experts. They may well have been working on the issue or theme for some time, perhaps privately with other subject matter experts and have joined the community, as they are keen to move things forward. Well that's the best-case scenario! In the worst-case scenario, you may find key contributors join to manage the contributions of others in the direction they want them to go. It is the role of initiators and facilitators to help stop this from happening. They will need to challenge the key contributors and help move things forward in a more neutral, open and generous way.

At their very best key contributors will be open and thoughtful and happy to share their knowledge and experience. It is also good if they are willing to share things they have tried in the past – what has worked and what has not – and work with a spirit of generosity and not from a defensive and controlling position. At their worst they can become over controlling, feeling threatened by others potentially 'showing them up'.

As a key contributor it can be galling to have people find solutions very quickly to issues you have been working on for some time. A disgruntled key contributor can threaten the life of the community, their subject matter expertise can be used to discredit, challenge and question the contribution of others. But to benefit from being part of a workplace community, key contributors need to let go of these feelings very quickly. The norms and culture of the workplace community that are set from the initiation stage can help with this. By demonstrating openness and directness, balanced with respect and support, the workplace community can collectively help manage the integration of key contributors into its work in a positive way.

Members – for your workplace community to be successful it needs to attract a diverse membership. People, who are interested in the theme, accept the scope of the community and feel they want to get involved. It is community members interacting with each other and key contributors that will start the process of making the community work. Members bring new views and ideas. They challenge the status quo and bring new insights to old issues. They can also point out things that might have been missed, highlight repetitive patterns and challenge outmoded thinking.

Community members' contributions will vary over time with periods of high activity followed by periods of lurking and watching. This is fine. Facilitators can help draw people in and encourage engagement. They can also help the conversation move and highlight what the workplace community, through engagement and interaction, has achieved.

Specialist roles

There are a number of other, specialist, roles, you may wish to establish and informally recruit for, to help your workplace community be successful. These people may not necessarily be members of your community but provide you, as the initiator, with advice and support as you need it. Again we would argue that these are not essential but can be very helpful. They include:

Communication specialists – they can help you with everything from the launch of the community, through to helping to shape the outcomes of the community into a form that the organization recognizes and will welcome.

Organization Development practitioners – they can help you understand group and social dynamics and help you decode what is happening in your workplace community. They can also support you in mapping the community's progression through to transformation. They can provide you with guidance on the use and development of interventions to support the community's healthy functioning. In addition and if needed, most good OD practitioners are good at facilitation, moderation and mediation. They may also have skills around knowledge management that you can tap into.

IT tools specialist – to provide you with advice on how to make the right choice and best use of the tools and technology you need to facilitate dialogue, capture knowledge, carry out polling and search the community for nuggets of information and such like.

Our advice when working with technology specialists is to follow the old UK Civil Service adage of 'specialists being on tap and not on top'.

That is, have their input driven by the needs of the workplace community, rather than by what tools and technology are available. In this way tools and technology will be fit for purpose and you won't end up shaping the community around the technology.

Human resource development **(HRD) specialists** – people with this skill can help community members make sense of what they are learning about themselves as community members as well as about workplace community ways of working. This includes issues of leadership and management as well as understanding the skills development needs that may emerge through community interaction.

Metrics specialist – In Chapter 9, we will show you how to develop a dashboard to help you gather, record and analyze metrics for your community. We will also show you how to develop measures that make sense to both community members and stakeholders. It may however be useful to have someone on hand who has an understanding of the wider organization's metrics to bounce ideas off about what and how to measure.

Metrics are an important feedback mechanism. They are important in terms of community members and in the wider organization, understanding that your workplace community is working as planned. They are also very useful in keeping the wider organization aligned with your work. Good metrics can be a reassurance to community members, helping them to track progress and understand what is working well and what is not working.

Launching your community – getting members

There are two main choices you have when it comes to launching your community and attracting members; a big bang launch or more of a stealth approach, with a soft launch and growing your workplace community organically. We will explore both of these in more detail below, along with their pros and cons.

Big bang launch – this has the benefits of getting the message and your invitation for people to join the community out there clearly and all in one go. Potential community members will understand what they are signing up for, the role and scope of the workplace community and what is likely to be expected of them. If you have a community sponsor then they may be able to help you with this. They can issue an invitation and promote the launch of the community as part of any regular communication activities they undertake.

The down side of the big bang launch is that it can over-identify the workplace community with the formal organization and, being top down, it can recreate the culture of control and hierarchy at the start of the community. Once a culture has been set it is very hard to shift.

You may also find that a lot of people who join, do so because they feel they have to, rather than through any strong desire to contribute. Given the size of the 'bang' at the launch they want to be part of it and not left out! It may be seen as the thing to be seen to be doing; a senior leader has said it's a good thing! This is the opposite of what you want. You want community members who have thought about joining and are doing so of their own free will. They are interested in the issue and feel they may have something to contribute.

A big bang launch may lead to it taking more time for the work place community to move from initiation through to coalescing. More time will need to be spent in the potential stage as the workplace community takes time to align itself and work out who really wants and needs to be part of it. The big bang, with accompanying communication, will have set high expectations, expectations that the community may fail to realise in the short term leading to disgruntlement and disappointment. We have seen several examples of these big bang launches, the members respond in the short term, with the initiators and sponsors believing it is a success, only for this to be shattered as the community fails to reach the maturing stage. Once the dust from the lunch has settled, there remains little contribution and energy. Having gone through this dramatic drop in contribution and energy it may be difficult for the workplace community to recover, survive and start to thrive.

We are not saying a big bang launch is a bad thing, just that you need to be careful how you manage it.

A soft launch – this is where you think through who you have in your network and from this identify those who you feel might want to be involved and who you believe will have something to contribute. You can also think of this as a collaborative launch, as you will be inviting people and then asking them to invite others who they feel may be interested and have something to contribute. They in turn invite others and so on. This is essentially a launch by word of mouth.

If you are planning a soft launch we suggest you carry out a quick and dirty form of network analysis to build your initial list of invitations. You can use the template below to help you with this (Table 4.2).

The positives of a soft or collaborative launch are that you are more likely to get willing participants and people who want to be part of the workplace community as opposed to those who feel conscripted, coerced or even forced into being part of the community. You are less likely to get people who are joining because it is seen as the thing to do and the place to be. The downside of the soft launch is that it may take longer to build membership and you may have to repeat the social networking exercise a number of times as well as getting community members to do it during the launch stage and encouraging them to invite people to join.

Table 4.2   Simple network analysis plan

Simple network analysis				
Community name				
Name	Current role	Interest level	Possible role	How to engage

As people join it is a good idea to welcome them as through your early interactions, you start to set the tone and culture of the community.

Planning the launch

It is well worth seeking the support of a communication specialist as you plan the launch. They will likely have ideas as to how to best craft invitations, and how to build plausible promise and express personal opportunity in the invitation.

We suggest you develop a launch plan using the following template (Table 4.3):

Table 4.3   Launch plan

Planning your launch		
Task	Help/How	When
Establish the scope of your community		
Identify and test your theme		
Agree your purpose		
Identify a name for your community		
Is anyone else working on this issue?		
How will people find out about your community? How will it be discoverable?		
Identify and engage with stakeholders		
Identify clear and hoped for outcomes		
How will you keep connected to the wider organization?		
How will you attract people to join?		
What basic processes do you need to develop?		
What tools and technology do you need?		
What roles will you need and how will you encourage people to take them on?		
Who can you test your ideas with?		

Community processes

When thinking about how your workplace community will work together it is important to be relaxed enough not to overmanage and overprescribe. In todays workplace we are used to fairly tight boundaries and rules. However if you overmanage your workplace community you are likely to kill it before it even gets started.

As a lot of your workplace community's activities are likely to be online and if your organization already has internal social media resources, by reviewing how people engage with this, you will get a good idea as to what behaviors you will potentially see within the community. It is well worth having a chat with whoever manages your internal social media to get their advice and seek their support.

Things to think through

There are some key things you need to think through about managing your community prior to launch and initiation. These include asking yourself:

• How do you expect people to work together in the community?
• What kind of interactions will you be looking for and encouraging?
• Are there certain behaviors you will discourage?
• Will you encourage or discourage simple social interactions?

We would suggest you see these as building social capital, that will help people to connect and learn to trust, and it will help them move quickly to working on the issues in hand.

'Chitchat' – on the surface this can look like a waste of time and a distraction. However we would argue that letting the community find its own level and being patient, waiting to see what emerges, is the best plan. If you do come to feel that nothing is happening and the community has simply become a 'talking shop' then in Chapter 6 we offer some suggestions as to what you can do.

• Will you develop a draft set of workplace community rules, a code of conduct of some kind? Or.

- Will you be happy to let the community emerge and allow it to set its own norms and establish its own ways of working?

Again the danger here is one of over-managing and in doing so, simply recreating the norms of the wider organization within the workplace community. Another danger with imposing norms is that they can end up driving out diversity and bringing in overconformity.

On the other hand a code of conduct can help people feel more secure. If your organization does have a social media manager we suggest you talk with them and see what is already in place in the organization to manage contributions on the intranet.

What we have found works well is, when things start to move away from the purpose and theme of the workplace community, asking community members how they think their current activities are connected to the theme and purpose of the workplace community?. This may be sufficient to get them back on track. Or they may challenge back and explain that what they are doing is important for the task in hand.

Workplace community members behaving badly!

One thing that often concerns people about workplace communities is what to do if people misbehave. In our experience this is a rare occurrence. Yes, it can happen, but it is much less likely than you think. If they do misbehave, or arguments happen, then the normal rules of human behavior and the wider organization's policies apply. If people start to exhibit bullying, sexist, racist, homophobic or other unacceptable behavior then the response should be the same as it would be if they were working together in the wider organization. In most cases organizations will have policies related to appropriate use of technology, security, social media guidelines, netiquette and harassment policies – in our experience these will in most cases be sufficient to handle any cases of misbehavior within a workplace community.

For more minor transgressions people need to be reminded that they are in the workplace community to support, develop and work on the topic in hand and not for personal point scoring or ego boosting behavior. They need challenging in the same way as would be done in any organizational or everyday situation.

As we said previously, from our experience, such situations are a rarity in workplace communities. It is however worth thinking through should anything untoward happen, how you would deal with it. You may want to explore this with your OD or HRD specialist. If behavior does go a bit off track, then what we have experienced is that the workplace community becomes self-correcting and community members intervene and redirect the energy of the community.

If you do wish to develop an online code of conduct then these are the kinds of headings you may wish to think through.

- What behaviors and or actions do you want people to exhibit and what behaviors would you proscribe?
- Are there specific organizational issues that are off topic and must not be addressed? Things that could be share-price sensitive?
- Are there any 'givens' you need to spell out to community members?

We believe that rather than having a long list of dos and don'ts and a complex code of practice that will need to be policed, you are better off setting the boundary conditions very clearly at the initiation stage of your community. You can then help community members navigate their way as they join in and engage.

chapter 5

Stages of Community Development

Introduction

In Chapter 4 we looked at what you need to do to get started with developing and building a workplace community. We looked at how to get traction in your organization and the roles you need to fill to get going and successfully develop and build a flourishing community. In this chapter we will share with you a model we developed and that we believe will help you understand the life cycle or stages that a workplace community goes through.

This model will provide you with a framework and road map to help you plan and understand what is happing to your workplace community from the time it is just an idea through to when the community has served its purpose and comes to the end of its life. For those working with existing communities the model will help you understand the stage your community has reached and what the next stages are.

Communities can revert to earlier stages in their life cycle, when significant events occur. You may find that your existing workplace community is not where you thought it was! We suggest you share this model with community members as it will help them develop a common language. It will also help them identify when things are working well and perhaps more importantly when interventions might be needed to move the community along and improve its functioning.

Getting started

At the beginning of our research we sought out people who had experience of being part of a workplace community and explored their experience with them. In many cases, until we spoke with them, they would not have thought of themselves as being part of a workplace community. They simply saw themselves as working cross-departmentally, cross-functionally or being members of a special task force or project team. However as we explored further and dug deeper, we were able to find examples of communities that had come together around issues of importance to people that were not tasked or formally commissioned by the wider organization. These were normally associated with technical problems and issues where the community members felt that the knowledge needed to address the issues in hand were not all contained in their department or silo. They wanted to tap into the collective intelligence of the whole organization.

How we developed the model

Formal, academic research into workplace communities is pretty thin on the ground. What does exist is a lot of work, research and good practice on community development in terms of social change. This work tends to focus on communities of place within civil society. Within this practice of social community development, there are two main approaches; those that are asset- or strength-based and those that are deficit-based. The best way of understanding these two approaches is to think of asset-based models as investing in the strengths of the community and deficit-based models investing in the problems and issues the community faces.

The example below will help you understand the difference between the two. Imagine a local community that has problems associated with poor housing, teenage pregnancy, youth crime and high levels of social depravation. Here is how the two approaches to community development would work.

A deficit-based approach

People with this frame of reference carry out research into the problems in the community and develop plans, usually top down, that involve

funding organizations and people they believe that can make a difference by working directly on the problems the community face. For
example, with regard to teenage pregnancy, they could fund campaigns
about sexual health. To tackle the high crime rate they could strengthen
the police presence and raise its visibility across the community. To raise
the levels of employment they may fund job clubs and work prepara-
tion schemes. In essence, they seek ways of funding the community out
of its problems and to fill the perceived deficit.

An asset-based approach

People with this frame of reference firstly look at the problems and at
the same time aim to understand and establish what the strengths of
the community are; trying to understand what the community is good
at and using this as evidence of what strengths it has. So, for example,
if there are a lot of young mothers in the community this might represent a community that has a lot of latent caring skills, if teenagers
are stealing cars, does this represent an interest in motor mechanics?
After a thorough analysis and a lot of engagement with the community
where these latent assets and strengths are identified, it is these areas
that are chosen for investment.

The approaches are very different in terms of beliefs and values.
However one common element they both share is recognition that
there is a need to invest in communities to bring about change.

What has this got to do with workplace communities?

Our bias is towards taking an asset-based approach and that is reflected
in the model we have developed.

We have always taken an asset-based view of organizations, communities and their development. This is because we believe it gives people
the opportunity to feel hopeful, yet realistic, about the future and we
find an asset-based approach encourages giving and generosity. Taking
a deficit-based approach is more likely to encourage people to play the
blame game and shift any responsibilities for change and development
away from themselves towards others. With a deficit-based mind-set it
all becomes the responsibility of leaders and managers and as such any

sense of personal agency is diminished. Deficit-based usually implies a 'victim' whereas an asset-based approach will usually lead to people taking more responsibility.

So when we started our research we took an asset-based approach and sought out those areas of the organization where people were already working in a nascent community way and learnt from them. We were seeking to build on what was already there in terms of interest, passion and excitement, rather than looking to inject these into parts of the organization where we perceived they were currently missing. We were following the old OD adage of 'go where the energy is'.

We would like to acknowledge the work of Etienne Wenger, Richard McDermott and William M. Snyder and their book *Cultivating Communities of Practice* (Wenger, McDermott and Snyder, 2002). In addition we were inspired by Bill Plotkin's Book *Nature and the Human Soul* (Plotkin, 2008). These books contributed to our thinking on communities and what their stages of development might be.

Predictable stages of community evolution

Having spent time observing and engaging with workplace communities we started to identify a number of predictable stages communities went through from initial conception through to healthy functioning and eventual decline. The model below is a culmination of that work (Figure 5.1).

The model explained

The model comprises a number of distinct stages. It is an evolutionary model that begins with processes of initiation and getting started and moves through to a final stage of transformation and choice. That is when the community has come to an end and either 'dies' or morphs into something else. As with all such models the work of one stage has to be over and complete before the community can move to the next stage.

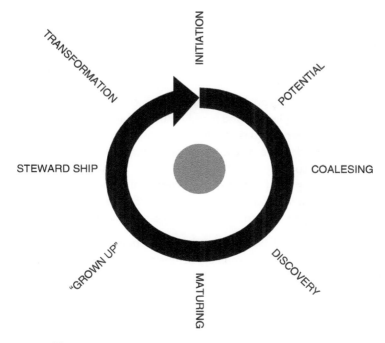

FIG 5.1 Community evolution model

One question we are often asked is how long does it take to transit each stage? From our experience, there is no fixed time that a community needs to or will spend at each stage; it can take a day, weeks, months or even years! How long transition takes will depend on the community's ability to do the work it needs to do to move between stages and what support it has available to it in undertaking this.

There is also no time dependence between the stages, meaning that the amount of time spent in one stage will not dictate how much time is spent in a later stage. A workplace community can become stuck in a stage for an extended period of time. It may never move on.

The following sections outline each stage in more detail.

How to use the model

The model can be used in a number of different ways, to:

- Plan activities to establish, cultivate and support the development of a workplace community
- Assess and map the progress of a workplace community
- Help community leaders and members understand what is going on
- Develop a shared language to describe their experience
- Identify and describe where things are going well and when problems have occurred
- Understanding what is normal for a community and yet outside the normal experience of individual community members
- Predict problems and issues that will need to be addressed.

To support this model, we have developed a number of diagnostic tools and interventions that community members can use if they feel their community has become stuck at a particular stage or problems have arisen. These can be found in Chapters 6 and 7.

Understanding each stage

In any grouping of people, team or organization there are always three key things going on:

Task – the practical tasks, activities and work the group or organization needs to do. What outputs and outcomes are they focused on. From building a ship, preparing a set of accounts, writing an encyclopedia developing an app or operating system, providing social care to the elderly, collectively developing a new business strategy, and so forth.

Structure – how work is organized and carried out. Do people work on their own or collectively, do people meet face-to-face or virtually, what equipment, tools, techniques or machinery do they use, etc.

Process – how do people work together on an interpersonal level. How is conflict handled, are people listened to. How do you contribute, is contribution rewarded and encouraged, is creativity encouraged or does the task simply require unquestioning repetition?

We extended and developed this model to help us explore and explain what we saw happening at the different stages of the development of workplace communities. Our terms are:

The task

These are the things the workplace community needs to do, for itself, during any particular stage of development, to move on to the next stage. As we define it, the task, is different from and should not be confused with the work the community has come together to undertake. Its purpose, function and scope. The completion of these community tasks do not happen by accident, but must be worked on consciously and purposefully by community members in order to make the transition.

The tasks of a particular stage have to be completed and this completion to be accepted and understood by all community members for the community to be able to transition smoothly to the next evolutionary stage. If a community is unable, for one reason or another, to complete the task then it will end up stuck in its current stage of evolution. If it attempts to move forward without completing the tasks of that stage, a lot of energy and effort will be wasted on trying to complete the tasks of the new stage whilst being trapped by the incomplete work of the previous stage. This will be a distraction from the work the actual community is trying to complete.

Focus

This is what the attention of the community is on at a particular stage, in terms of social and psychological focus. This is how we know what stage a community is at. As the community focus shifts we know the community has carried out the tasks of that stage and is about to move to the next stage of its evolution.

Contribution

This is the outcome of the work that the community, as a whole, is doing for the wider organization and the value it is adding from this particular stage of its development.

Roles

Here we detail the roles the community needs to be successful at any particular stage and that are needed to help it transition to the next stage. These do not need to be dedicated roles and can be shared amongst community members. Some do however require specific expertise, others are much more general.

What can go wrong?

Each stage has its set of own unique challenges. In this section we will help you to understand the challenges, how to identify them and what to do to overcome them. We have a number of very practical interventions that will help you. These are detailed in Chapter 6.

Metrics and return on investment

We will deal with measuring the overall effectiveness of workplace communities in Chapter 9. Here we will explore community measurement in general, the development of community return on investment (ROI) and a scorecard and how to monitor and manage the process of measuring success.

Stage 1 – initiation

This is the stage where you decide whether or not a community way of working is right for you. Will it work with your organization's context and will it address the issues you wish to work on? During this stage, through engaging with others, you will have the opportunity of testing your ideas and experimenting with a community way of working.

As a way of getting going we suggest that you share this book or extracts from it, with people you wish to involve, either directly as community members or those who need to give license and permission to your experimentation.

We have also developed a launch planning template which you will find in Chapter 4.

The task – is a community the right thing for us?

The task of this stage begins with deciding if a community way of working is the best way of achieving your objectives and desired outcomes. In Chapter 2 we introduced you to a questionnaire to help you assess which way of working would work best for you. We suggest you use this to help you decide if this is the right approach for you. You may also find the following questions helpful in leading you to the right decision:

- What do we need to do and what choices do you have about how you achieve this?
- Is the issue or task in hand one that you can do on your own or do you need help?
- If you do need others involved what would be the best or ideal way of working together?
- How easy will it be to get people involved?
- How easy will it be to find them?
- What ideas do you have about how to launch the initiative?
- Can you interact in a face-to-face way or will you need online, social media technological support? If so what sort of interactions do you anticipate you will need (sharing, co-creating, conversations, announcements, etc) and do you have the tools and technology to enable this to happen?
- Who else needs to be involved and who needs to give you license or legitimize it?
- What kind of governance would your community need and how easy will it be to put this in place?
- Given the objectives and governance, what is the expected level of decision-making and authority within the community? How will decisions (if any) be made?
- What has already been attempted (if anything), what can you learn from the success, challenges of earlier efforts?

We suggest you first answer these questions for yourself and then engage others in discussion around them until you build a consensus about whether or not the issues you wish to work on are ones that are best suited to a community ways of working.

Focus – do we believe this will work for us?

The focus of this stage is around individual and collective belief that something is possible, that the issues to be addressed are important enough for us to give our valuable time energy and effort to them. Potential community members and those in governance roles need to believe that something is possible; is it plausible, are we trying to boil the ocean? And they need to believe that their contribution will be meaningful and worthwhile. They need to understand the connection between their commitment and the impact it will have on the wider organization, the responsibility this entails and the possibilities that working in this way will have for their own development.

Contribution – passion and ideas

People connect with others and share their passion for ideas and possibilities when they share intent, belief, resources, preferences, needs and risks, resulting in a common identity and sense of purpose. In doing so they start to develop new thinking and ways of conceiving the issues in hand as well as how to work together. For the organization, the contribution is the opening up of new possibilities for ways of working and the development of new thinking and practice about how work needs to be organized and managed. We don't need to do things in the same way they have always been done!

What can go wrong?

There are a number of things that can go wrong at this stage. These include:

- Choosing a workplace community way of working when it is not appropriate to the task in hand and another way of working would be best suited to getting things done.
- At this stage it is easy to become obsessed with technology and tools. These are enablers to community and not 'necessary conditions' for the successful initiation of a community. Tools and technology have their place, but should not drive the agenda when making choices

about whether or not a community is right for you. Avoid making this a technology exercise.

• Not finding the right people to engage with. This can include not knowing where to look or not being able to reach and engage people in a dialogue around either the task or issues you wish to address. It can be challenging to know who within the organization is interested, perhaps already working on the task or issues you wish to address; let alone getting people interested in a different way of working, which may require them giving up exclusivity or control.

• Not being able to frame an igniting question, a call to action, or to clearly communicate the intent. That is being able to frame the plausible promise, the challenge you wish to work on in ways that excite and interest people.

Roles

These are the roles we believe you need at the initiation stage:

• The initiator, someone who can frame the issues and understands enough about community ways of working to be able to explain it to others and build interest.

• People who are interested in the issue in hand and are willing to give their time to explore the issue and are open enough to explore new ways of working on it.

• People with OD and or community development experience who you can bounce ideas off of and whose expertise you can use in bringing people together to help facilitate the sharing and harvesting of ideas

• People who have an understanding of technology capabilities, collaboration tools and social media on hand to provide advice on how to facilitate online communities and also develop knowledge management systems for gathering, saving and sharing wisdom.

Stage 2 – potential

Once you have passed through the initiation stage and decided that a workplace community is worth the effort and likely to achieve the desired outcomes, and worked out how it will add value to your organization and support to those who join, your community has potential! It is now time to move into the testing stage to see if this potential can be realized.

The task – testing

During the testing stage it is important to find out if there is enough common ground to connect people. Is there a common understanding of the bargain, what's in it for me either explicitly or implicitly? Do they see the value of sharing their insights, stories and knowledge about the issue in hand? Are they willing to make the effort to support the community to allow it to get started?

To navigate this stage you need the energy to find others who are interested and have the ability to talk them through both the issue in hand and how this new way of working will enable them to move things forward. People need to understand how their passion, energy, and enthusiasm will translate into something meaningful, worthwhile and useful; both for themselves and for the wider organization. It is vital to ensure that people are joining through their own free will and not being coerced into being part of the community. Communities will not work for long with pressganged volunteers!

Energy and enthusiasm are vital but are not enough. The community needs to understand how to translate this into action. For potential to be truly realized, people need to have a way of contributing, whether this be face to face or technologically. Tools and technology are critical and essential for a virtual or geographically distributed community. The technology needs to be easy to use and fit for purpose. The last thing you want is for people to get bogged down by the technology and forget the issue in hand. If this happens it will quickly drain community members' energy and commitment, and become a major stumbling block.

Focus – inquiry

The focus of attention at this stage is on people exploring the issue and confirming, through inquiry, if it is real and meaningful to them and the wider organization. Is the 'plausible promise' sufficient for them to put their time and energy into working on it?

It is important for the community to have an open culture, one that allows and even encourages people to ask what may seem like irrelevant or even silly questions. People need to feel sure that this is something they wish to get involved with and can only do so if they have an authentic opportunity to inquire and find out. They may also need to make appropriate challenges to the issue and whether a workplace community is the best way of achieving results.

Contribution – seeking

Through processes of inquiry and being supported and encouraged to do this, potential community members will move into seeking mode. This provides them with a sense of adventure, the kind we feel when we are starting a journey to somewhere we have never been before. We may not know where we are going but the very act of getting involved and setting off can raise our spirits.

Through inquiry, we can find out if we are seeking the answer to something that is important to us and also start to tap into our natural generosity. People will need to know and understand that they are seeking not just on behalf of the organization or others but that there is something in it for them. Community ways of working, as they cross boundaries and provide people with a high degree of autonomy in terms of how and when they engage, can reawaken a new spirit of adventure, one they may have been lost as people engage in their day-to-day programed and prescribed activities at work and at home.

What can go wrong?

Passion is not enough to make a community. There has to be something real for people to engage with and contribute to. If passion is all there is then it is likely that after an initial rush of excitement, people will start to disengage and leave. The work of the community has to turn interest into something useful that community members can see has an impact either on themselves or on the wider organization.

Sometimes it may not be possible to find the right people with the right level of interest or the passion needed to make time to be involved with the community. People just may not be interested enough. The issue may not connect with them.

As we have already said, tools and technology are not the driving force of a community, however they are important in that they facilitate dialog, sharing and engagement. If you have the wrong tools, or tool-phobic members, this in turn will limit community members' ability or desire to inquire, explore and test the potential for this way of working. Remember to avoid technology for the sake of technology.

One of the hardest things for anyone initiating a community to do is to let go and allow the community to self manage. We all have a tendency to want to over-manage and over-control! It's a bit like baking a cake, putting it in the oven and then opening the door every five minutes to see what is going on. As community initiators and leaders we need to develop a sense of trust. At times it is important to intervene, but these need to be guided judgment calls. It is important to establish the conditions in which the community can self manage. Starting to let go is critical at this stage.

People coming together to address one issue through a workplace community can sometimes get overexcited and see this way of working as the answer to everything and end up wanting to 'boil the ocean'. This becomes a distraction from the main issues the community has been set up to address. If this is not properly managed people can become trapped by the potential of a community and not achieve what they initially set out to do.

Roles

During this stage, in addition to the roles from the previous stage, community initiator, facilitator, OD practitioner and someone with expertise with social media and collaboration tools, you also need to identify key contributors and a core group of influencers.

Stage 3 – coalescing

If you are able to navigate successfully through Stage 2 – potential, the next stage you enter is coalescing. This stage is about bringing it all together and starting to work as a community for the first time.

Task – coming together

During this stage it is time to review the launch of the community and to see if it has worked. The detailed metrics we have developed and that are included in Chapter 9 will help you with this. However you can tell easily by looking at the kind of activities in the community. Are they meaningful? Are they the kind of things that build relationships and trust? Are the topics proving to be engaging and exciting? Are they enough to catch people's imagination and want to make them get involved? Do people know what and how to share?

At this stage you should start to see norms and rules beginning to emerge, and it is important to track these and see if they are enablers or if they are getting in the way and stopping contributions.

Focus – shared belief

This stage is all about developing a shared belief in both the issues the community wishes to work on and a community way of working. The focus of the group should be on developing shared beliefs and the culture of the community. To do this, community members need to operate from the beliefs that they have the skills and experience to address the issue and by coming together can realise the potential these offer collectively to create something new and wonderful. If the community feels they don't have the skills they need then they need to find ways of encouraging those with the skills to join.

Contribution – finding

At this stage the contribution the community makes to the individual and the wider organization can best be summarized as; they have found a group of people who have a passion for the same topic and a critical mass who are enthusiastic about moving things forward. They also have the collaboration tools and techniques in place to allow for the release of this passion and make a difference.

What can go wrong?

Lots of noise and no real activity. The community is busy but the focus is scattered with no sense of a coming together around issues of importance. People make a lot of comments but little by way of original contribution to move things forward. They also do not know how to see through the 'noise' and can't find what may be weak signals that have the potential to lead to greater understanding and development.

Lots of people lurking. The community has a lot of members but very little activity or activity that is not of very much value. People are curious, interested about what is going on, want to be part of something but are not contributing. The sense of purpose or topic is of interest, but they feel, for a number of possible reasons, they are not able to contribute.

Things become exclusive. With people not being encouraged to join in or engage in the topics at hand. A small group can emerge that intentionally or unintentionally keeps others out and becomes 'exclusive'. This is especially common in a community that has a lot of subject-matter experts, when people who are not considered experts join and try to engage.

New ideas are not encouraged. People are working to a preconceived script and see anything else as going off topic. The community becomes a place where people just rehash old ideas and complaints, rather than looking forward and exploring what may be possible. Open criticism of a new idea, particular by a community leader, can significantly reduce the possibility that others will share new ideas.

Infighting can emerge. This is usually focused on ownership. Whose community is it? People set too many rules and boundaries and things become overly bureaucratic and in effect the community starts to be a reflection of the formal organization.

People feel they are subject to rather than citizens of' the community. They look to develop a hierarchy and want to know who is in charge and have that person tell them what to do.

The community can become 'cult like' that is, the rules become self explaining and the community becomes a closed system. In essence the community becomes a bit like the flat earth society! Despite all the evidence to the contrary, people hold onto and promote unsustainable beliefs.

Roles

At this stage you should see key contributors emerging. These will not be fixed roles and may shift over time, as different kinds of expertise and input are needed. Of course you will need 'confirmed' community members, people who are engaged and involved on a regular basis. The community will also have a number of 'loose' affiliates. People who will come and go and contribute as they feel able. They may not be as fully involved as the core group of key contributors.

Stage 4 – discover

The task – commitment

It is during this stage that you find out whether or not the community approach starts to deliver or not. This is also the stage when if the community is not delivering you can use a range of diagnostic tools and techniques to find out why not. You can then choose to intervene, be patient or close the community. Choosing to close the community is likely to be based on you finding out that this way of working is not able to address the needs in hand.

So what does success look like? During this stage you should see interest and enthusiasm being turned into true engagement and co-creation. You should already be able to produce a list of things the community has found out; in terms of new things the community has discovered and the confirmation of things you thought you already knew. You can also test out the energy levels of community members. What kind of contributions are being made and how frequent are they? What is the tone of the contributions? Do you detect excitement or resignation? In terms of leadership has it become hierarchical? Has a queen bee emerged, or is it shared and operating in more of a heterarchical way? That is, leadership is moving between community members depending on the issues and topics being explored or tasks the need to be carried out.

Are people drifting in and out of the community? If they leave do they come back and do you know why they choose to leave or move from contributors to lurkers? Typically people will leave a community by not contributing and not even lurking. It is a mistake to think that if the number of registered members does not change very much you have a healthy community. Community members may well have remained registered but are 'resigned on the job'.

It is also interesting, at this stage, to find out what is being said about the community inside the wider organization. What kind of attention is it getting? Are people talking about it in a positive way? Is it seen as relevant and useful or a distraction from the main work of the organization? Do people think it is contributing to success and part of the future or simply a waste of time and a messy distraction?

Fundamentally is the community simply a talking shop? Or has it found out something new and has it already started to make contributions to the wider organization, being recognized as a good and positive thing?

Focus – identity

At this stage the community will tend to be identified with and defined by the topics it is working on and not yet by the outcomes it has achieved. People are driven by the desire to discover and are not yet fixated on outputs and outcomes.

Contribution – realism

Community members begin to understand the difference between the true possibilities of doing something new, developing new ideas and approaches and boiling the ocean. Reality about what can be achieved becomes dominant and drives out or dispels any fantasy community members may have had about saving the world. It's not that saving the world is a bad thing. It is more about a recognition that this has to happen one step at a time and workplace communities, although a step in the right direction, can only ever be one piece of this. However a common sense of fighting against the world, a sense of revolution, can be a powerful driver of contribution.

What can go wrong?

At this stage the ease with which people can use collaboration tools and technology is of vital importance. If the tools are over complex, don't work or have become over dominant then they can drive out the possibilities for real sharing and engagement. People will get frustrated with them and most likely leave and not come back.

People can feel overwhelmed by what they see as the size and scope of the challenge. This can lead to apathy and disengagement, driven by feelings of being overwhelmed. The work the community is doing can be experienced as being too hard. People can feel daunted by the size of the task and a feeling that this is a long-term engagement. They may not be up for this level of commitment.

What people have found out is perceived as not being worth the effort. They feel they could have done it more quickly on their own or by working in a different way. In this situation community ways of working are considered a distraction and a waste of time.

Roles

At this stage it is good to find some partners in the organization, who are not part of the community, but who know about it and its aims and aspirations and are able to offer external reflections, thoughts and ideas. A 'critical friend' who can let you know how the community is being perceived and what you may need to do to make sure it is positioned appropriately and recognized for what it is and what potentially it can do.

Stage 5 – maturing

As your workplace community moves into the maturing stage you will experience a sense of settlement. The community will feel established and becoming a norm in terms of how people work in the organization. As the community matures, then focus, roles, boundaries and ways of working become clarified and are no longer the focus of much discussion. It is also easy for community members to induct new members into being part of the community.

The task – confirmation

The community has achieved a sense of stability and can grow and change from this. Rather than constantly emerging and re-emerging from the flux present at earlier stages. This is not to say that there is no complexity, it is just that people now understand and, with experience from earlier 'growing pains', know how to manage and navigate through these with ease and elegance.

By this stage the wider organization will have started to recognize the value and contribution the community is making to the workplace and the organization's overall strategy, goals and targets.

As the community matures it needs to balance moving forward with still being open to new people, continuing to grow in size and manage the process of inclusion.

It is also important to establish whether people still feel truly connected to the work of the community. Are they still engaging with it, moving things forward and making new discoveries?

Contribution

In our experience at this stage people begin to feel a new sense of hopefulness about themselves and the wider organization. We believe this is as a consequence of either their own generosity, through contribution being rewarded by learning something new or through experiencing the generosity of others. At this stage community members often find that their relationship with the wider organization starts to change for the better. It can heal past issues and help them to see the wider organization in a new light.

What can go wrong?

During this stage there can be a tension between older members of the community welcoming and engaging with new members. Older members may feel that new members are taking them back to issues they have already addressed. Wanting to renegotiate rules and norms that they feel have already been set in place and are working well. This exclusivity can lead to the process of community becoming more important than the work the community is doing. Ending up with community for the community's sake.

As the community becomes mature, people may feel the need to start institutionalizing roles, responsibilities and ways of working. This is not always a bad thing. However we believe it is important to keep things fluid and open enough to allow for new discoveries and creativity. If the community becomes too fixed, mirroring the wider organization, it runs the risk of losing its usefulness and ability to make a difference.

During the mature stage, it is also important to keep the bargain the community is offering its members clear and in the forefront of their minds. If the bargain changes significantly it will change the dynamics of the community and impact on contribution. Community members who have been previously active contributors may well stop contributing all together.

To mature, community members need to be able to move fully into feeling and acting like citizens of the community rather than feeling subjects of it. As citizens, people operate from a position of shared ownership and a sense of collective autonomy. Requests of others are invitational in nature and not commands. As subjects people tend to wait for others and to be told what to do.

If the community has transitioned to maturity then community members will have developed their own ways of navigating what on the surface can appear to be confusion. They understand how topics shift and move, how leadership is being managed and is appropriate to the task in hand. If there is still a high level of confusion in the community it means that the norms and culture have not been understood and or have not been properly shared and bought into. It could also mean that they are not appropriate to the role and purpose of the community and need to be reviewed and changed.

Roles

At this stage it is a good idea to connect with experts in the field of communication, people who can work with the community to help it represent its work and outcomes to the wider organization.

Stage 6 – grown up

This is the stage where the work of the community translates into real benefits for the wider organization. The community starts to deliver results and positive outcomes and these are directly attributable to the community and recognized as such. The wider organization can see the value of the work the community has done and continues to do. Community members can also see and understand the difference their work is making.

On a personal level community members are also able to start to understand how the experience of being a member of a workplace community is enriching their work life and helping them develop new skills and capabilities. At the same time, they will also have developed a wider understanding of the organization as a whole and know how to contribute to the whole rather than in a partial way, or driven by a job description.

The task – progress

During the grown-up stage it is time to stop tinkering and decide if the way in which the workplace community is working is fit for purpose. Is the community good enough for what it needs to achieve? It is time to stop an endless quest for perfection that might be underway. The community now needs to be open enough to take feedback from those outside and react in a thoughtful and considered way, rather than with any kind of defensiveness. Grown up also means translating the thoughts and ideas of the community into suggestions and associated practical action plans. During this stage the community should feel an increased pull from the wider organization and this traction will allow it to start making requests for things like additional resources and opportunities to carry out experiments and implement its findings.

One of the challenges of the grown-up stage is balancing the need for the community to be open to further exploration, whilst at the same time harvesting what has already been done. The community will be moving into a business-as-usual mode and one of the challenges here is to maintain the excitement and interest of all involved.

Focus – achievement

Community members will begin to recognize that it is possible to achieve extraordinary things by working in this way. Success, both personal and organizational, does not rely on the organization's formal structures and processes and there is real power in using workplace communities to address organization issues. Such a realisation is also likely to impact on community members' personal management approach and style outside of the community and make them more considered in how they exhibit personal leadership.

Contribution

The organization and community members will start to see clear outcomes for their work. They will understand the power of generous co-creation as a way of addressing organization issues and developing and delivering something new.

What can go wrong?

People can get trapped by the process and lose focus on the outcomes. That is, the process of the workplace community can become too engaging in and of itself. Exploring ideas and discovering something new can become addictive! Sometimes we don't want this stage to end and feel constrained by having to focus on outcomes and implementation.

The community can become so inward focused that it loses connection with the wider organization. If this is the case then it will be hard to gain traction for ideas and suggestions that come from the community and any recognition for contributions the community may have made.

Communities can become closed to new ideas and can also resist any input from external sources. A 'not invented here' mentality can arise. Community members feel their work is so special that unless you have been involved from the beginning you would have no way of understanding what it is all about. The outputs of any work can also be seen and felt to be so precious that community members do not want to let go and they resist any attempts to share work for fear of losing control.

The community can become all-explaining and feel it has all the answers and therefore has no need of others. It becomes reluctant to share outputs. This can lead to it being very difficult for others to gain entry to the community.

Roles

There are no new roles required for this stage. However the community initiator and facilitator are key to helping steer the community in the right direction and guide it towards delivery.

At this stage any emergent roles will be well understood. Individual members' reputations will have been established through their contributions and interactions.

Stage 7 – stewardship

This stage is all about sustaining the community over time and supporting it in maintaining its relevance to the wider organization and to its members. It is also about ensuring that the voice of the community is being heard and that appropriate and relevant recognition and rewards are given to the community as a whole, as well as individual members for their contribution. People should feel proud to be part of the community and of the contribution the community is making to the wider organization.

The task – development

Communities that remain static die, or without interest and participation they slowly drift away. To continue they need active stewardship. This is a task for the community as a whole and not just the community facilitator or leader. The key question to address is what can the community do to sustain momentum and energy? This involves building on what has already been accomplished and developed. It is vital during this stage that feedback loops both inside and outside the community are kept open and the community is kept connected to the wider environment. The very act of seeing how the work of the community is impacting on the wider organization will help to keep the community alive. Stewardship is all about maintaining this link and drawing community members' attention to the impact they are having on the wider organization and on each other. In doing so this helps to build an appetite for on-going activity and development.

Stewardship may also involve the community reinventing itself and shifting its focus to new issues. In turn this may also involve recruiting and welcoming new members to the community as well as saying goodbye to old members. Without active stewardship the community can become closed, stale and trapped in the past.

Contribution

During stewardship, community members should get a sense of their own innovation, contribution and influence. This can come from either inside or outside the community. Recognition from community peers for work well done, for exhibiting generosity and achievement will help to keep people engaged and active. Feedback is vital at this stage. Feedback from the wider organization is also a key element in helping people to recognize the value of their work and make them want to continue with it.

What can go wrong?

People may feel the community has become too institutionalized and that they have lost the sense of freedom they felt when they first joined. This is often a consequence of roles becoming over clarified and the community being held too tightly with norms that say what is right and what is wrong. Things feel over formalized and the confusion often associated with creativity is not encouraged or tolerated.

The creative actions of the group are held in closed spaces and not open to the community as a whole. This stops open participation or engagement. Lurking, which can be a pre-participation activity, is frowned upon and challenged. There can be calls for these lurkers to be removed from the community since they are perceived as being of no value.

It is hard for new people to gain entry, learn the rules and start to contribute. Contributions from new members may not be welcome. The community ends up relying on a few old stalwarts who tend to be over involved, over engaged and over committed.

Roles

The key roles here are those that keep the community connected to external stakeholders and keep these stakeholders committed to and interested in the community.

Stage 8 – transformation

During this stage community members need to decide if the community in its current form still has a relevant role to play and should continue, or is it time for it to close and die or time to transform into something else?

The task – transformation

Now is the time to ask if the community has started to fade away and is it losing members and energy. Has its original purpose died and left in its place infighting or low levels of contribution with very few people showing up?

Have things become so institutionalized that more time in being spent on community processes as opposed to true community activities like co-creation, creativity and the sharing of ideas and knowledge? Has the community become a drain on resources with little or no discernable output? Has the bargain fundamentally changed, are contributors now demanding something different for their continued contribution? Has there been a radical shift or change in leadership or facilitation? Is it now time to move away from a community way of working into something more traditional like a center of excellence or formal organization? Would this serve the organization and the community members better?

Focus – limbo

It is highly likely that people will feel change coming. They will remember the excitement of the other stages and know what they have been able to deliver but somehow now they feel stuck in limbo, waiting to see what happens. They are not very sure as to what lies ahead and are trying to get the energy together to find out. At this stage there is likely to be and fond discussions of the past and more talk about the health of the community and whether it is worthwhile continuing than there is actual work focussing on wider organizational issues.

Contribution

Community members know they have been successful in the past and they remember and acknowledge their own and others' contributions to this. They are also likely to be more reflective about what they have learnt and how the experience of being a part of the community has developed them. They often feel sad that things are different now and changing. But if it's a healthy community they may also be having feelings of excitement about the future and satisfaction about a job well done. They are also conscious of what they have learnt in terms of skills and abilities and will feel that their capabilities and personal capacity have been enhanced. They will know that no mater what happens they can take this with them. They are also likely to have made new connections, new relationships and friendships that can be further developed and leveraged outside of the immediate confines of the community.

What can go wrong?

People can find the transformation of a workplace community very difficult especially if it means the end of an exciting part of their work life. This can force them back into wanting to be subjects and told what to do, rather than being active citizens shaping their own destiny. They can start to become dependent and begin to project their anxiety on to others, individuals or parts of the organization. This can lead to people becoming angry when they don't get the answers they are looking for, even if there are no answers to give at the present time. If this continues they can start to feel victims of the community.

Sometimes the work of the community is done, complete and finished or business reality has shifted and the topic no longer has relevance or in essence the topic has died. In these cases it can be extremely hard to have people let go of it. They have invested their time, effort, energy and generosity in something that was important to them and they felt part of. Experiencing it as no longer being important can be devastating and takes careful managing.

Roles

External stakeholders who can validate the work of the community and thank people for their contributions

Summary

This model provides you with a framework to help you understand the stages involved in the workplace community life cycle. If you are initiating a workplace community, it will provide you with the roadmap of activities that you can follow as you start your community development journey. If you already have a community it will help you to understand the current state of that community, and what lies ahead. We will refer to this model throughout the remainder of this book.

6

What Can Go Wrong?

Introduction

In this chapter we will explore what can go wrong with your workplace community along with some ideas you can use to get things back on track. In Chapter 7 we will provide you with highly practical tools you can use to resolve the issues we identify in this chapter.

In Chapter 5 we shared a model of workplace community evolution that we believe will help you understand the stages the community will naturally go through. We also highlighted some of the things that can go wrong during the different stages. Issues that will hold back your workplace community's evolution and get in the way of it functioning effectively and reaching its full potential.

Functional or dysfunctional?

Workplace communities are a very new way of working and you may find it harder to understand or read what is happening in the community. Much more so than when you are trying to understand or read what is happening in a more traditional organization. It can therefore be much harder to tell if the process is working or not. Unlike a hierarchical organization or a project, in a workplace community there is no set of default status reports to keep you informed and no direct reporting lines to manage issues through. The patterns of interaction and behavior within a community can be measured, see Chapter 9. However, as you will see in that chapter, you need to think about this in a different way.

As you have made it this far in the book, you will have started to develop an understanding of how and why workplace communities work, what success looks like and what it will look like if a community is not working. As with anything new, we need to calibrate ourselves and develop familiarity with what is going on. It is very useful to be able to test and share your perceptions with others. This will stop you either panicking, thinking it is all going wrong, or missing the signs that some form of intervention may be needed.

What may look to be dysfunctional in a hierarchy may be perfectly normal and helpful in a workplace community. For example, in a hierarchy people are normally discouraged from challenging authority in an explicit and direct way. Within a healthy workplace community leadership is a shared function that moves between and amongst people. People find it easier to appropriately challenge and take on the mantel of leadership if they feel that this will move things forward. However issues can arise and the community becomes dysfunctional if people are not willing to take on leadership roles or hold on to them too tightly and are unwilling to let others take over when it is appropriate (Figure 5.1).

What evolutionary stage are you at?

One of the first things to do is to identify what evolutionary stage your community is at; what stage is it going through? As well as using the model in Chapter 5, you will find Table 6.1 useful in helping you with this. In Table 6.1 we have taken each stage and broken it down into:

Personal – what people will be experiencing, the kinds of questions they are likely to be asking themselves and what they are seeking on a personal level from their engagement with the workplace community

Interpersonal – how people will be interacting with each other and what is likely to be driving these interactions

Table 6.1 Community evolution assessment tool

Workplace Community Assessment

	1. Initiation	2. Potential	3. Coalescing	4. Discovery	5. Maturing	6. Grown up	7. Stewardship	8. Transformation

Personal	**Will this be interesting and useful?**
	• Curiosity
	• Does it capture my attention?
	• Will it be useful?
	• Who else do I know who might join?
	• How much time will be needed?
		Will I be Accepted?
		• Who is here
		• What role can I play?
		  – Leader
		  – Contributor
		  – Fact Finder
		  – Lurker
		• Feel uncertain, tentative
			Am I needed?
			• What ideas, experiences and expertise can I contribute
			• Do I agree or disagree?
			• What is in it for me?
			• The credentials game
			• What do I like? Dislike? Accept?
				What is here for me?
				• Who else has joined
				• Is the purpose what I thought it was?
				• Do I believe it will make a difference?
				• Can I contribute enough and in the right way?
					How can I help the group?
					• Here is how I would do it
					• Feel comfort or discomfort about the role I am playing
					• Want to help
						How do we keep going?
						• How do I maintain my contribution and interest?
						• Am I getting more back than I ever thought! More than I am giving?
							Are we making a difference?
							• Getting feedback
							• Ideas for development
							• Validation of effort
							• Personal recognition
								Will I be forgotten
								• What happens next?
								• Will friendships last?
								• Will you be useful to me in the future?
								• What's next for me?
								• How will I be recognised?
								• Have I secured my reputation in new ways?

	Inquiry • 'Sniffing' around • Questioning • Checking out who is there • Lurking	**Politeness** • Small talk • Generalities • Limited disclosure • Relationships begin to form • Toe in the water	**Bid for power** • Who will lead? • With whom can I align myself? • Compete with others on personal agendas • Flight or fight • Quiet apprehension	**Who is here** • What do people know? • How are we sharing? • Who is missing? • Is there enough common interest?	**Co-operation** • Self disclosure • Here is how I do it • Recognizing others ideas • Listening more carefully • Commitment to emerging leadership	**Adult to adult** • Trust, openness and understanding • We belong here • This is the place to do great work • It is okay to ask for help	**Recognizing** • Sharing success inside and outside of the community • Building external relationships • Acknowledging what we are achieving	**Sadness** • Will we work together again? • What's next for us? • How do we share success? • Can we recreate the excitement we used to have around • Something real?
Inter-personal								

(Continued)

Table 6.1 Continued

			Workplace Community Assessment				
1. Initiation	**2. Potential**	**3. Coalescing**	**4. Discovery**	**5. Maturing**	**6. Grown up**	**7. Stewardship**	**8. Transformation**
Invitational	Orientation	Organizing	The bargain	Information flow	Business as usual	Keep on keeping on	Memory
• Openness • Connections • Personal • Relevance • Authentic and real	• Why are we here? • What do we want to achieve? • Identifying strengths of the group • Skills and capabilities – what do we need?	• What is the real problem? • Resistance to others ideas • What is our mission, goals and strategy • How will we proceed? • Are the right people here?	• What do we give what do we get? • Is it worth it? • Is the bargain clear? • Will this make a difference? • What does the organization think?	• Open exchange of ideas and information • Problem definition • More trust • Urgency to identify, evaluate solutions	• Sustainability • Trust is evident • Openness • Tolerance of people and ideas	• Connecting outside • Making an obvious difference • Validating outputs and outcomes	• How will our work be remembered? • Will our contributions last over time? • Shifting from the past to a focus on the future

Community

Community – what is the community driving towards as a collective? What is the whole as opposed to the parts?

We suggest that you share this table with members of your workplace community as an aid to discussion. This will help all members develop and build a shared understanding of how the community is evolving and developing. In turn this will help community members develop a shared language about what is going on and help them calibrate themselves to this new experience. It will also be a great help in analyzing what is happening if you start to feel that things are not working, as they should.

It is worth remembering that people may initially feel that they are in different places in the cycle. However in our experience after some reflection and through using the table people will find that they are broadly coalesced around the same stage.

Questions to ask

Assuming you have been able to identify which evolutionary stage of development your workplace community is at, the next thing to do is to ask yourself the following questions:

- What is happening, what am I seeing and how do I feel about it?
- Am I happy with how things are going or feeling uncomfortable?
- What is it like being a member of the community? Is it an enjoyable positive experience or has it become a chore?
- What 'corridor conversations am I hearing about the community? What are people saying about it? Am I happy with what I hear?'
- Can I begin to sense what will happen next?

It is also a good idea to ask members of your community similar questions to help you calibrate your experience with theirs. Questions like:

- How do they feel about being a part of the community?
- What is working and what is not working for them?
- What would they like to see more of and less of?
- How easy is it for them to contribute?
- What will keep them contributing and what will drive them away?

Depending on the answers to the questions above, you may want to seek some help in making sense of things. This would be a good time to have a chat with an OD practitioner. You can talk through your findings and any concerns you have. They should be able to help you get clarity and to plan you next steps.

Involving the community

As someone who has initiated a workplace community it is very easy to feel completely responsible for its health and well-being. In traditional organizations we all look to our managers and leaders to sort out organizational ills. However in a workplace community the responsibility for the successful functioning of the community rests with all its members. Your role as a community initiator is to provide the space and sometimes the tools to help the collective understanding of what is going on and come to agreement as to what to do about it. This is part of everybody's role and not only yours. You don't have to do all the heavy lifting on your own.

Action inquiry versus expert interventions

When trying to understand what is happening in your community we suggest you follow an 'action inquiry' approach. By this we mean, carrying out a process of inquiry both 'with and for' the workplace community. The opposite of this would be to play a more traditional consultative role using expert power. Playing 'doctor patient' with your workplace community where you are the doctor and the community is the patient. There is nothing inherently wrong with doctor patient interventions. However these are likely to go against the spirit of a community way of working. Community members will feel something is being done to them and that they have little input or control over this. We believe, and would encourage you to as well, that the spirit of a community comes from community members feeling a sense of shared ownership of what is happening and work together to achieve success.

With an action inquiry approach you work with community members to help build a shared understanding of what is happening and then co-develop ways of addressing any issues you have identified. This does not mean that you cannot use expertise or any special skills you may have. What it does mean is that you don't jump to conclusions without checking these with community members. The best way of initiating this is to start with inquiry followed by reflection and finally to agree actions.

Some workplace communities decide to seek expert help to support them and help them make sense of what is going on. Another approach we have seen work very well is for the community to designate a facilitator or facilitators, whose job it is to look after the community, and to pay attention to what is going on and intervene as needed. In Chapter 4 we explore workplace community roles in more detail.

So what can go wrong?

The rest of this chapter will be devoted to a series of scenarios describing what you might be experiencing in your community and what to do about it. In Chapter 7 we will explore the individual tools in more detail.

Context

In writing this context for the scenario we have kept it organization type and workplace community theme agnostic. It is not that we lack imagination; it is simply that we don't want people to feel excluded if the organization type does not match their own or their theme or the scope, and so forth.

The community

You have launched a workplace community, following the guidelines we have given in earlier chapters. You spent time thinking through and working out the scope, theme, purpose, name, plausible promise and bargain. You carried out a stakeholder analysis and garnered support for this new way of working from critical stakeholders. You undertook a quick and dirty social network analysis to identify who you know and who might also know people who would have an interest in the work of the community and may wish to join and get involved.

You identified a set of in-company tools that could be used to enable the community and developed a launch plan. You have found some personal support in the form of a tame IT specialist and an OD practitioner who are interested in new ways of working and who you feel will be able to contribute to the successful functioning of the community.

You have developed a launch plan and feel confident you have all the bases covered. All in all you are feeling quietly confident that you are ready. This should be an interesting and hopefully successful experiment that could lead to some exciting findings and potential change for the organization. These are some of the things you may experience:

Nothing happens

Nothing is happening. Despite your best efforts only a very few people, or in the worst-case scenario no one, has joined! Or, another variation on this, people have joined but nothing is happening. There is no interaction, no inquiry and no contribution. You feel disappointed and a bit hurt. You have put a lot of effort into setting this up. You have built it, yet no one has come or the ones that have come are not the right ones! You feel a bit embarrassed, as you have staked your reputation on introducing a workplace community and it looks like it is not going to work. You have made commitments to your stakeholders and can feel their beady eyes looking over your shoulder! Your sense of panic is rising! You are not sure what on earth to do!

Things to do

First of all

Look at the evolutionary stages guide and at how we describe the initiation stage. Double-check your induction of community members plan, is it rigorous enough, have you truly launched your community?

Ask yourself 'have I properly inducted new members?' Review what you did to launch the community, how personal will it have felt to those invited to join and ask yourself have you done enough? The key question here is 'have I really launched'?

If you are happy that you have launched properly and the members are the right people then the next step is to go back and review your answers to the ways of working questionnaire'. Run the questionnaire again and ask your supporters to do the same. Would your issue be better suited to another way of working such as hierarchical, a project team or some other form? Review the outcomes. If this confirms that a workplace community is the right way of addressing your issues then review your scope, purpose theme and so forth. Restate these if necessary. Decide if the best thing to do is to re-initiate and re-launch your community.

Tools and technology issues

Your community is active and people are buzzing, but mainly about the tools and technology that are there to support community activities and are not the theme or purpose of the community. The buzz includes complaints about the tools not working, lack of functionality, people moaning they are overly complex, and some community members undertaking an obsessional search for the best tool with other community members pushing their pet tools. You hear people saying that only tool X will make this work and the community mangers need to get their act together and demand funding to buy this. Over time this becomes iconic and the lack of tool X becomes linked to a perceived lack of commitment on the part of the organization to invest in and address any and every issue, not just community tools.

You feel extremely frustrated; as tools were the last things you thought the community would get fixated on. You had imagined that your fellow community members would make do and the theme and scope would drive the community. Not an obsession with technology. You also know that, in the current economic climate, to go to key stakeholders with a tool-shopping list and a request for resources to fulfill this, would be futile. This kind of expenditure, and on something that people see as at best experimental, is not going to be greeted very warmly. It will impact on your credibility and by association the credibility of community ways of working.

Things to do

Carry out a few in-community experiments yourself with the tools and ask a couple of trusted community members to do the same. You need to work out if people's complaints are founded in reality or are they a side issue that has become an easier issue to work on to avoid the main theme of the community. It is not at all unusual for people to deflect their concerns and anxiety about one issue onto another. One that feels more manageable to them and does not require them to confront issues that are more difficult to address and require more personal risk to raise. Complaints about tools can become a displacement activity.

If you do find you have tool problems, such as the tools are not reliable or too complex to use, then you will need to address this issue. This is where you need your tame IT professional to help you.

However if your tests show the tools, whilst perhaps being a bit clunky and not as easy to use as they might be, are fit for the purpose, then you will need to intervene in the community.

Before you intervene have a look at what people are saying and not saying. By not saying we mean by focusing on the issue of tools what are they not focusing on? Do you detect a sense that the obsession with tools is actually displacement activity as described above? If it is, you a have couple of choices, which one you choose will depend on your level confidence. You may need the support of your OD practitioner to help you with this.

Firstly, you can confront the community head on. You can tell them that these are the tools you all have and there is no chance of getting any additional resources to build a new platform. Basically telling them to get on with it! We have seen this stating of 'the givens' working very well and getting people back on track. Secondly you can use the data you have gathered to confront community members with how their constant banging on about tools is a displacement for something else. Tell them what you suspect the something else may be. Be open to being challenged back. If you do this in an appropriately careful way you may find that people will shift their attention from tools to the real issues. Again you may need help with this. Thinking through how to frame your challenge in a way that helps people think and reflect on what they are doing, rather than simply antagonizing them.

Of course if the worse comes to the worst, you can always join in the chase for the perfect tools and start engaging in displacement activities yourself!

Remember there will always be a better tool out there, be it a new version, an upgrade or a totally new platform, chasing the perfect tool is likely to become an eternal quest!

The wrong members?

You have launched your workplace community and there is a lot of activity and a real buzz. You feel very happy and perhaps even a bit self-satisfied and self-congratulatory! You are looking forward to talking to those stakeholders who were very skeptical and showing them! Yes it works! However when you start to look a bit more closely and listen in, there is a lot of noise but not much going on. All there is, is a lot of chitchat and gossip. People exchanging ideas and thoughts about anything and everything, from sports clubs, where to eat the best food in Tokyo and how awful the movie *Titanic* is! People just don't feel interested in the scope, let alone the theme or purpose. You seem to have plenty of plausible promise and people still want to join. Your workplace community is seen as a cool place to hang out! But is not seen as a place to do any real work.

Things to do

Check what stage of development your community is at. If it is one of the early stages then you can expect more gossip and chitchat than in later stages. People are testing themselves and each other and looking for people they can trust and feel comfortable with. It is quite normal for people to engage in community small talk as the relationships between members develop.

Have a look at how you have constructed and presented your scope and theme as well as how you have framed the issue. Are they clear and focused? Have others look at them to see if they are compelling enough to help people focus. Make changes if required and then gently restate them to the community. Congratulate community members on their level of energy and invite them to focus their energy on the theme. It is also an idea to check by carrying out a poll in the community, to see if the theme, scope and issues capture people's attention and they are willing to focus on it. Chapter 7 contains examples of polls you might wish to use. You can also ask community members for help in reshaping the issue and reframing the scope and purpose.

Ask people what their expectations are and what made them want to join in the first place. Have community members share this with each other. In this way you can start to build interest in the theme and start to build momentum towards it. Through sharing you are also building a sense of community though people understanding each others' expectations. It may also be an idea to revisit you social network analysis and review who you have connected with and invited to join. Specifically work with those people you believe to be key contributors, have private conversations with them and request their help in getting things going. Carry out the exercise again and invite new people.

Also review your induction and how you welcome people. Is there a way of using this process to get people to focus more quickly and build buy-in?

What's going on?

You are very happy with the level of engagement and activity in the community. However, you are finding it hard to keep track of what is happening, to capture learnings, ideas and thoughts. You feel worried that if you are not keeping an eye on things and keeping track of every conversation and interaction then you will lose something or miss out on something exciting! You find yourself constantly checking, lurking and engaging. To the point where you are missing out on other things in your life!

As in physical communities, there will be a public and a private side to your workplace community. People will say certain things in a public forum, other conversations and interactions will occur one-to-one or within a sub-group of the community. It may well be worth checking with the people you believed to be key contributors, asking for their perception of where the real conversations are happening.

Things to do

Explore the possibility of undertaking sentiment analysis on community activities and dialog. Sentiment analysis is the analysis of feelings behind the written words using natural language processing tools. These tools look beyond the numbers of posts, depths of threads, counts of words, and interpret what people have written. There are many tools on the Internet available for this, most widely used to assess and understand the impact of social media marketing. In the basic form sentiment analysis will identify the positive, natural and negative sentiment of the dialog within your community.

Have a look how you are structuring knowledge management in the community. Are there any formal or informal systems in place? If not, open up a discussion about how the community feels it is best to capture its learning and outputs. Also check with your tame IT specialist to see what knowledge management and interrogation capabilities your tools have. Make sure that community members know that these capabilities exist and how to use them.

Beware of the four following things: firstly over managing what is happening. You will see a clear difference between idle chitchat and people using chitchat and gossip as a way of settling into this new way of working. Remember the metaphor of the gardener from Chapter 3. Secondly, beware of getting over-invested in the workplace community. Thirdly managing outputs and outcomes is a shared activity and not solely your responsibility. You may need to remind community members of this. And finally, remember you do have a life outside of the community and don't forget to enjoy this!

Exclusivity

You feel very happy, as things have been going well and according to plan. You have been able to track the stages using our guide and the transition between stages has gone well and not been too bumpy. You have only had to intervene a couple of times and this has been mainly to offer support and a bit of clarification. However you feel concerned as you are starting to see that a few people are beginning to dominate the community in ways that don't feel quite right. You decide to wait a while and see what happens.

As you lurk a bit more, you notice that people are finding it hard to gain entry to conversations and discussions and are being excluded. You notice that after trying once or twice they just give up. You know that the strength of the workplace community depends on its members and by that all members. Good ideas, insights and the stimulant for creativity can come from anywhere. If an 'in group' forms that means you will end up with an 'out group' as well. Out groups tend to get bored and leave.

Things to do

The first thing to do is to check your perceptions with others. Talk them through with few trusted community members. It can also be a good idea to approach one or two of the people who you feel have been excluded as well as a couple of those you feel are actively excluding. However tread carefully and do not make too many judgments at this stage. What you are seeing may not match the experience of those in the community. Your perception could be wrong. What you may be seeing is an appropriate corralling of work to provide space for people to take something to more depth. There may be no intention to exclude on their part, simply a need for a bit of peace and quiet whilst ideas are developed prior to being offered back to the community for further work. These are perfectly natural processes but ones that sometimes people are clumsy with and so it may look like exclusivity but in effect it is simply the search for a bit of peace and quiet. However if you do find that it is exclusivity and exclusion then you need to act fast.

We suggest you use the health of your community index in the next chapter. Invite people to complete the questionnaire and then give feedback on the results to the community. This kind of feedback may be all that is needed to stop this issue. However if it does not stop, then you may well need to have a direct conversation with the people at the heart of the issues, those who you and others have experienced as excluding, pointing out how their behavior is not helping the community and nor is it within the spirit of this way of working. You can also show them how their behavior is having negative effect on the health of the community and is likely to impact on the community's ability to achieve its purpose and fulfill its potential. Be prepared, they may choose to leave in a huff!

Over-control

Something strange seems to be happening in the community. You notice that increasingly two or three people are acting as gatekeepers. Before anything happens people are checking with these people if it is OK. You have also seen evidence of these gatekeepers increasingly acting as queen bees giving their blessing to some activities and not to others. You can see how other community members are spending a lot of time second-guessing them and trying to please them. It is not that these people don't have skills or capabilities its just that they seem to be exercising a lot of managerial authority in the group that seems to be limiting the options of others to contribute.

Things to do

As ever it is important to check that your perceptions are shared and that you are not making assumptions or over-interpreting. The behavior of these people may be enabling the group to focus and your perception of them gatekeeping may just be temporary. Check with others and in particular those you feel may be acting in a subservient way and giving away their power. Use the 'subject to citizen' checklist to see to what degree people are feeling like subjects of the community as opposed to fully empowered citizens. Feed the data you gather back to the community, stimulate a discussion and ask people what they think needs to happen to create the kind of workplace community where everyone feels empowered.

Infighting

You feel a sense of despair, as community members cannot seem to agree on anything. One says black and the other says white! You can see a lot of infighting going on. While this will usually create a lot of energy and activity in the community, it feels like these fights, turf wars, arguing about unimportant issues are poisoning the community. People have moved away from having appropriate and healthy professional disagreements. These have become personal attacks. There is a lot of 'he said, she said' blah, blah, blah!

Things to do

We suggest you use the sense of community index or community health diagnostic to raise the issues. It might be an idea to talk with your OD practitioner and have them help you review the norms you have either encouraged through a code of conduct or that have emerged during initiation and potential.

Feedback the norms to the community along with your analysis of the responses to the sense of community or community health diagnostic (whichever one you use) and ask community members how their behavior fits with these. How is their behavior helpful to the achievement of the community's purpose and scope.

It is important to make this intervention in a timely manner. Members not directly engaged with the infighting will not find the community a place to be while this is ongoing. It may provide 'entertainment' in the short term, but after a while it become boring and will poison the community spirit.

Having intervened, keep a close watch. It is quite usual for such heated disagreements to be re-kindled at a later stage and you may need to intervene again.

Stalled?

Your community has been running for a while now. You have been really happy both as a member and also as the initiator. Some very interesting and helpful things have emerged and you are getting very positive feedback from the wider organization to the work the community is doing. However in the last little while nothing new has emerged. The community is starting to feel a bit stale and turgid. You are beginning to wonder if things have come to an end and no one has told anyone!

Things to do

Review your scope, check what stage you think you are at and ask yourself and the community if its work is over. Use the evolutionary stages guide to check what stage the community is at and to see if it has got stuck at a particular stage or has it made it to transformation stage without you noticing? Check your perceptions with the wider community. If it has reached the end of its life then it is time to begin the process of closure. Just raising the prospect of closure can either re-ignite the community to work on the original scope or cause a transformation.

Inward focus

You start to feel a sense of unease as you experience people interpreting what is going on in a very fixed and rigid way.

That is, you have seen people explaining why things happen or why they cannot happen in terms only of what is happening within the community. The community has become self-explaining, self-referencing and inwardly focused. Data from the outside world is routinely rejected. There is a strong sense of them and us and it's 'us against the world'! You can see that the 'them' is the wider organization and the 'us' the community. You can see people talking about how the community is the only place they feel understood or truly part of something. The wider organization seems to have become the 'big bad wolf!'

Things to do

Have a look through the cults checklist; does this reflect in any way what you are seeing? Share the checklist with the group and have them reflect on it. If needed involve your friendly OD practitioner to help you address this issue. You may also think about re-stating the purpose of the community and also exploring ways of connecting the community back to the wider organization. One way of doing this is to re-share the expectations of stakeholders and make it clear that there is a symbiotic relationship between the workplace community and the wider organization and not a parasitic one. You can also share with them stories of what happens in cults – perhaps starting with the drink the Cool Aid story of Jimmy Jones and the Jonestown massacre....

The boss finds out!

Things are jogging along very nicely and the community is doing some interesting work. You feel quietly confident that you have done the right thing in initiating the community and are looking forward to being able to share the outcomes with the wider organization. You are also learning a lot and are enjoying the process. That is until you get an email from one of the organization's senior leaders. Basically, the email is asking you what the hell is going on and why are employees wasting so much time engaging in pointless activities that have nothing to do with their day jobs. You gulp!

Things to do

Firstly don't get mad, feel defensive or start a fight! Remember what we said about stakeholders in Chapter 4. A stakeholder is anyone who has or feels they have a legitimate interest in the work you are doing. The key word here is 'feel' they have, even if you believe they should mind their own business and let you get on with things.

Have a look back at your stakeholder list and check if you made any contact at all with them prior to the launch of the community. Are any of your supportive stakeholders connected to them and able to offer you support in managing your relationship with them. Check to see who in the community is connected to this stakeholder. Talk with them about their relationship and how best to manage their expectations. Then gird your loins, rehearse your elevator speech and book a meeting.

Over-inflation, boiling the ocean

As you talk to others in the wider organization you are hearing some strange things being said about the workplace community. People are extremely positive and very excited. In fact perhaps a little bit too much so! They are expecting the community to achieve the unachievable. You get the impression that the burden of delivery on the community may be too heavy.

The community has produced some interesting ideas and outcomes, but it is early days yet. You have heard a number of senior leaders say, 'Oh lets have the workplace community look at that...' or 'I am sure the workplace community will come up with some great ideas that will help us...' You begin to fear that the next challenges for the community will be to bring about world peace, quickly followed by finding a cure for cancer and then terraforming Mars....

Things to do

All your actions should be about managing expectations, both within the community and in the wider organization. Tread carefully. You don't want to kill excitement and passion. Help people become realistic and at the same time not lose their spirit of excitement. Revisit your stakeholder list and book some meetings. Check to see how their expectations have shifted. If they have become a bit overexcited then calm them and help them become a bit more measured.

Stimulate a discussion in the community about what is realistic and at the same times what people truly feel they can achieve. Help them understand the difference between their dreams and practical reality.

Offer to hold some lunch-and-learn type briefings in the wider organization about your experience of initiating a community as well as being a community member. Use these as an opportunity to encourage a hopeful yet realistic view of what outcomes there might be.

Drifting

You are finding it hard to read and understand what is going on. People are doing their own thing and going off topic. Some are showing a distinct lack of commitment to the work of the community and others don't seem to understand what is going on or what is expected of them. It all feels a bit muddled and chaotic.

Things to do

Use the buy-in benchmark with the community to explore this. Have them rate where they think they and their fellow community members are and seek advice from the group as to how to get community members to move to being people who are happy, willing and able to champion both he work of the community and the process by which this is being undertaken. You may need to restate the community's theme, scope and purpose in a way that people fully understand what the community is about so they know what they are committing to. You may also need to re-state what the community is not about so people can make a choice about whether the topic is for them and they want to commit time and energy to it. Help people understand that there is no shame in leaving the community if they lack interest or energy for the topic in hand.

It's the end

For any number of reasons you and many other community members feel the community has reached the end of its life. Its work is done and yet people won't leave! People have had such a great experience that they are not wanting things to come to an end. They keep refining outputs and outcomes and have no idea that sometimes 'good enough is good enough'. It is hard to get them to let go, say thank you to each other and goodbye.

Things to do

Use the after action review process to formally review the work of the community and allow for closure. Help people to understand what they have learnt across three distinct dimensions. What have they learnt about:

• The issue, theme and topic
• Themselves
• Workplace communities

It is good to capture these learnings as you and others can use them to refine the initiation and management of future workplace communities.

Plan a celebration and seek ways to get the work of the workplace community recognized in the organization. Show how this could never have happened at all, or with the outcome achieved and cost effectively without this new and innovative way of working.

Set a date for closing the community allowing people enough time to say thank you and goodbye.

7

Putting it Right!

Introduction

In the last chapter we explored what can go wrong with a workplace community and provided you with ideas and suggestions as to what you can do to put it right. We mentioned a number of checklists, tools and interventions that we have developed and that we believe will help you to put things right and keep them on track. In this chapter we will share these with you and show you how to use them.

Nature of the tools, checklists and interventions

We believe these are easy to use and pretty much self-explanatory. Many of them take the form of checklists or inventories. You can use these for your own reflection and to help others make sense of what is going on. We encourage you to share and use them with community members, to help them develop a reflective approach and a shared sense of responsibility and ownership for the development and health of the community.

In Chapter 6 we also explored the nature of interventions and encouraged you to frame your thinking about how to intervene in a participatory, rather than a more hierarchical doctor versus patient way. By interventions we mean the kinds of things you need to do to make sure your community keeps on track and is a healthy environment for community members. Do keep in mind our gardener analogy; these interventions are intended to help you to assess or change the conditions in your community.

In Chapter 5 we introduced you to the idea of using the three elements task, process and structure as a way to analyze what is going on in the community. Some of our tools focus on one specific element; such as getting clarity on the task or surfacing process – that is what is happening in the community on a human or interpersonal level and may be getting in the way of its members contributing. Others look at a combination of all three. In the OD world we see interventions as structured sets of activities that will improve the performance of the workplace community and at the same time increase social learning. Through this process of learning, the workplace community will increase its capacity to take care of itself and develop its capability to self-manage.

Using the tools

We encourage you to use the tools to truly inquire into what is going on and not come to knee jerk conclusions. It is important to inquire into what is going on, develop a shared understanding of this and build both agreement and commitment to action. If you work with your workplace community in this way you will find that the healthy functioning of the community becomes a shared responsibility and all the weight will not be resting on your shoulders. The workplace community will shift from being 'your community' to becoming 'our community.'

The tools explained and explored

In the following pages we will explore each of the tools in more detail helping you understand how to use them and what to do with the outputs. The tools can be used with face-to-face workplace communities as well as for online use with virtual workplace communities. We believe they are pretty much self-explanatory and are designed to be easy to use. As such they do not require specialist's skills. However you may find it very helpful to work with an OD practitioner to use the tools, make sense of the outputs as well as develop appropriate action plans. Feel free to change and tailor the tools so they work best for your particular workplace community.

Diagnosing the stages of community development

This tool is your primary guide to understanding what it means to be a member of a work place community and to make sense of the experience (Table 6.1).

Purpose and use – to help workplace community initiators, members and key stakeholders understand the different stages a community naturally goes through along with what they will feel and experience at each stage; personally, interpersonally and across the wider community.

The tool provides a map community members can use to track, understand and manage their experience of being a member of the workplace community. It will help them build a common language to share their experience with others. Helping them to recognize when things are on track and when they are going off track. As the community moves between stages, this tool will guide community members and help them understand the transitions.

We suggest that you share this tool as part of the initiation stage, introducing it to people as they join the community and as part of their induction or on-boarding processes.

Process – share the guide at induction, ask people to read and reflect on it. Provide them with space to ask questions for clarification. Ask them if they feel it needs any amendments and additions to reflect the nature of the workplace community you are launching and the wider organization you are all part of.

Ask community members how they feel this should be used? Is this something that should be regularly reviewed to ensure community members are all on the same page and know what is going on? Encourage community members to keep it in mind as they work together and use it to help each other make sense of their experience.

Outcomes – community members have a base level and shared understanding of what it is like to be a member of a workplace community. They know what to expect and they have an easy way of interpreting their experience. If they feel confused about what is going on they can use this tool to check their experience and check this out with others. The community develops a shared language by which it can interpret and understand its experience. People feel connected by a common understanding of what is going on. They understand that the community will transition and evolve as it develops and what this will look and feel like.

Next steps – reviewing and reflecting on the outputs. If it appears people perceive themselves to be scattered across different stages then the following intervention will help community members coalesce around the stage they are really at.

The nine elements of effective community

This tool will help you to Identify and clarify what needs to be in place as you initiate your community (Table 7.1).

Purpose and use – A nine-element checklist to ensure that you have thought of everything you need and can initiate and launch your workplace community in a clear and systematic way.

Use this checklist to help with your planning and during initiation to validate your plans. We suggest you share it with community members, as part of their induction and on-boarding, to help them understand the thinking that has gone into the development and initiation of the community. They can use this to validate your work and also identify what else might be needed to ensure a successful launch. By working through the list community members will gain a greater understanding of what is expected from them. This checklist can also be used with stakeholders to help reassure them that you have thought things through. Again they may also help you identify things you have missed or that reflect the specific context of the organization.

Table 7.1   The nine elements of effective community

Element	Description		Rating	Identified actions
1. Appropriate leadership	• Community leaders have the skills and intention to develop a community approach. • Leadership is seen as a shared function. • Many are given the opportunity to exercise leadership when their skills are appropriate to the needs of the community.		0 1 2 3 4 5	
2. Suitable membership	• Community members are individually qualified and capable of contributing to the mix of skills and characteristics that provide a diversity of input. • The community is open to new members who bring new skills, ideas, challenges and thinking. • This is welcomed by all.		0 1 2 3 4 5	
3. Commitment to the community	• Community members feel a sense of individual commitment to the aims and purpose of the community. • They are willing to devote personal energy to building the community, and supporting community members. • When working outside the community, they feel a sense of belonging and are happy to represent the community. • The community has developed a climate in which people feel relaxed, able to be direct and open and are prepared to take risks in order to achieve their purpose.		0 1 2 3 4 5	
4. Achievement	• The community is clear about its objectives, which are felt to be worthwhile. • Energy is mainly devoted to the achievements of results, and community performance is reviewed frequently to see where improvements can be made. • The community recognizes its collective as well as its individual objective.		0 1 2 3 4 5	

(Continued)

Table 7.1 Continued

Element	Description	Rating	Identified actions
5. Wider organizational role	• The community has demonstrated that is has a clear, distinct and productive role within the wider organization. • It maintains appropriate connections with the wider organization and receives recognition for its activities • Relationships with other communities are well developed and people move freely between different communities as they feel the need.	0 1 2 3 4 5	
6. Effective work methods	• The community has developed lively, systematic and effective ways of working and is able to solve problems together. • It has processes in place that enable it to reflect on its way of working and is able to adapt to meet the needs of new members and challenges. • Roles and clearly defined interaction patterns are well developed, and administrative procedures support a community approach	0 1 2 3 4 5	
7. Critique	• Community and individual errors and weaknesses are examined, without personal attack, to enable the community to learn from its experiences.	0 1 2 3 4 5	
8. Self awareness	• Community members bring strong individual contributions. • Members have a good level of self awareness and know what they can do and what they need to learn. They are committed to the purpose of the community and help others work towards this.	0 1 2 3 4 5	
9. Creative strengths	• The community has the capacity to create new ideas through the interaction of its members. • Innovative risk-taking is rewarded, and the community will support new ideas from individual members or from outside. • Good ideas are followed through into action.	0 1 2 3 4 5	

Process – share and then score the extent to which you believe the condition currently exists – 0 = not at all, 5 = to a large extent. Discuss the checklist and scores with people, both inside and outside the workplace community. Reflect on how these roles and dimensions are currently present or not in the wider organization. If they don't exist in a healthy way in the wider organization then you may find it difficult to surface them in your community. Explore how you might do this in terms of task, process and structure. Be clear on what may be missing and how you can develop this or prepare for the likely impact it not being present will have on the healthy functioning of your workplace community.

Outcomes – clarity on what may be missing and what you can do about it. A shared understanding in the community as to what will help it succeed and what might get in the way; attention being paid to structure and process as important elements of community development. It is not all about the task! Without appropriate community infrastructure the workplace community is likely to struggle to achieve its aims and fulfill its purpose. The lack of infrastructure can become a pebble in your shoe that people become fixated on, rather than focusing on the work the community needs to do to fulfill its purpose and the outputs expected from it.

Next steps – add identified actions to your community development plan. Seek solutions to what is missing or develop ways of working around the issues as appropriate. Share your findings with the wider community. You can also revisit this at any stage of the development of your workplace community.

Community health diagnostic – General

Identifying where you and your workplace community might need help (Table 7.2)

Purpose and use – to help you and community members identify areas where your community needs help and support. We suggest you

Table 7.2   Community health diagnostic – general

Issue	Question	Answer
Membership	To what extent are the members included in workplace community activities?	
	How do people include/exclude themselves?	
	How do people include/exclude others?	
	Are there sub-groups within?	
	Are the right people here and are they participating?	
Influence	How do people influence others?	
	Who is most influential? Who is least influential?	
	How are decisions made?	
	How is leadership exercised?	
Climate	What kind of atmosphere exists in the community? Has this changed?	
	How open are people in expressing: • Their thoughts and opinions? • Their feelings?	
	What level of trust exists?	
Infrastructure	Are people making use of the available tools and technology?	
	Does the community have 'open channels' with the wider organization?	
	Are critical stakeholders actively supporting the community in general and community members specifically?	

use this after Initiation during the Potential or Coalescing stages. This will give community members the opportunity to reflect how things are going and if any problems or issues are starting to emerge. These can then be dealt with early, rather than leaving them to fester. This tool takes a bit of time to use as it required personal reflection and group discussion. Community members may need a bit of help with identifying what to do next. You may wish to draw on the support of an OD practitioner.

Process – there are a couple of ways of using this. Firstly you can start with a process of self-reflection. Score the instrument, using a similar

1–5 scale as used above, and then share the instrument with your workplace community and seek their validation and comments. Or you may choose to share the instrument with the community, collate the results and comments and feed these back to the community. You can then use this data to encourage further discussion and garner suggestions for actions to help the community maintain or improve its health.

We suggest you use this tool at planned intervals to help people understand that maintaining the workplace community's health is something that requires ongoing activity and thought and is a shared activity. Its not all about you!

Outcomes – a clear understanding of how the workplace community is doing, and agreed and planned actions. You will also be building a shared way of thinking about community health and a shared understanding of what this means in practice.

Next steps – an agreed and shared action plan that the workplace community feel they own and are responsible for.

Detailed

This is an alternative and more detailed tool with this focusing more on the health of your community. However both serve a broadly similar purpose and you can choose which one will best serve your needs (Table 7.3).

Purpose and use – to help you and community members identify areas where your community needs help and support. We suggest you use this after Initiation during the Potential or Coalescing stages. This will give community members the opportunity of reflecting how things are going and if any problems or issues are starting to emerge. These can then be dealt with early, rather than leaving them to fester. This tool takes a bit of time for personal reflection and group discussion. Community members may need a bit of help with identifying what to do next. You may wish to draw on the support of an OD practitioner.

Table 7.3   Community health diagnostic – detailed

Healthy	Score (1–5)	Comments
Optimism, hope and 'we are in this together'		
We can do it		
Value intangibles like vision and values		
Consensus building		
Polarization		
Collaboration		
Generosity		
Focus on the future		
Interdependence		
Broad community participation		
Leadership renewal		
Think and act in long term		
Listening		
Reconciliation		
Win-win solutions		
Politics of substance		
Diversity and involvement		
Inclusion		
Challenge ideas		
Problem solvers		
View challenges as opportunities		
Unhealthy	**Score (1–5)**	**Comments**
Cynicism		
Nothing works		
Emphasis only on tangibles		
Confrontation		
Debate the past		
Parochialism		
Few do everything		
Same old faces		
Short-term thinking		

(continued)

Table 7.3   Continued

Unhealthy		Score (1–5)	Comments
Attacking			
Hold grudges			
Win-lose solutions			
Politics of personality			
Challenge people			
Blockers and blamers			
See themselves as victims			
Scrooge-like – only me			

Process – There are a couple of ways of using this. Firstly you can start with self-reflection. Score the instrument and then share the instrument with your workplace community and seek their validation and comments. Or you may choose to share the instrument with the community, collate the results and comments and feed these back to the community. We would advise you not to take averages but rather to share the distribution of the results. You can then use this data to encourage further discussion and garner suggestions for actions to help the community maintain or improve its health.

We suggest you use this tool at planned intervals to help people understand that maintaining the community health is something that requires ongoing activity and is thought of as a shared activity.

Outcomes – a clear understanding of how the community is doing and agreed and planned actions. You will also be building a shared way of thinking about community health and understanding on what this means in practice.

Next steps – an agreed and shared action plan that the community feel they own and are responsible for.

Clarifying community roles

Understanding the roles in a workplace community, what they are and what they do (Table 7.4).

Table 7.4 Clarifying community roles

Role	What they do	True/False
Executive sponsor	Invests in the community with an expectation of benefit	
	Gives permission to people to use their time for the community	
	Provides guidance for community topics and sponsors community topics in leadership forums	
Community leader	Provides leadership to the community. Provides people and other resources to community and follows up workplace communities performance	
	Provides meaning and visibility to the benefits of the workplace community to its stakeholders	
	Provides coaching and guidance to community core team	
	Responsible for business performance and contribution of the workplace community	
Community facilitator	Helps the community to focus on its domain, maintain relationships, and develop its practices	
	Guide the community towards its target by helping to focus, delegating and encouraging/empowering	
	Recruit, interview, persuade potential community members to join & stimulate contribution	
Community member	Participates in the community, different level of activity among members (core group, active members, peripheral, outsiders)	
	Peer evaluation of person's competences, experience, contribution and performance	
	Knowledge sharing, competence co-development	
	Co-creation	
	Community maintenance and development	
IT support	Provides and configures the community tools and work space	
	Sets up any access controls and access mechanisms	
	Establishes technical processes and procedures	
	Provides technical support and advice on new features and functionality	
OD practitioner	Helps you to understand what is going on within the work place community and supports you in using interventions to maintain its health	
	Provides you with facilitation support as needed and acts as a mediator and trouble shooter as required	

Purpose and use – To provide you and community members with a clear understanding of the roles needed to enable your community to function successfully, the key elements of these roles and what they entail. We suggest you use this to check that you have all the roles you need and that these are being delivered in a way that is enabling for the community. In addition you can use this to recruit people to the roles and help them understand the nature of the roles and how they shift and change as well as what is expected of them and how to deliver on this.

Process – prior to initiating this intervention, review the roles description sheet. Check that it covers all the roles you think you need. Think through how easy it will be to identify community members who can take on the roles as you initiate and launch the community. This is also something to share with your stakeholders as they are likely to have suggestions as to whom you might approach, people who could initially take on these roles.

Given what we have already explored about the nature of workplace community roles, remember, these roles are more fluid than in the wider organization. They are often shared and can transition between people. In a healthy workplace community, community members will shape them so they are doable in the context of your specific community and fit in with their level of commitment. They will put their stamp on them and make them their own. In the wider organization roles have a much more rigid and fixed form of expression, being driven by job descriptions and fixed tasks and targets. Think through how, when using the clarification process, you can help people understand how these roles are more fluid than in the wider organization and are often shared.

You may find it helpful to include a version of this information as part of the induction and on-boarding process. Making it explicit what roles are needed and how the process will work. You can use this as a checklist for discussion in the community if you feel that people are not fulfilling their roles or you find that roles are lacking.

Outcomes – an understanding of what roles are needed and how these will be recruited to and acted on. People readily and enthusiastically taking on and delivering on their roles and helping to move the workplace community forward. A plan for how to manage role recruitment and engagement

Next steps – an action plan for recruiting to roles, a way of measuring role effectiveness and giving feedback to holders of community roles. A way of tracking and capturing how roles shift, transition and change over time.

Head, heart and hands analysis – Identifying yours and others' gifts

This tool will help you find out what you and others bring to the workplace community. We have developed this exercise from the gift exercise commonly used in asset-based community development (See Asset-Based Community Development Institute, School of Education and Social Policy, Northwestern University) (Table 7.5).

Purpose and use – to help potential and actual community members to understand and connect at a personal, individual and shared level with what it is they bring to the workplace community in terms of:

- **Head** – what they know and understand, intellectually from their past work and life experience. This includes not just what they know but also who they know and can either invite to the workplace community or access and use as a community resource
- **Heart** – where their passion lies. The energy they will bring to the workplace community and how happy and willing they are to express support and generosity
- **Hands** – the practical things that they can contribute and are willing to do, to enable the workplace community to achieve its aims

We suggest you use this as part of the initiation of the community and for the induction of new community members. Induction of new community members is an on-going process as people may join at any stage of community's development.

Table 7.5   Head, heart and hands analysis

	Question		Answer
Introduction	Who are you and what do you do?		
Gifts of the head	Who do you know who could help with this issue, inside and outside of your organization?		
	What past or present experience do you bring?		
	What do you hope to learn?		
Gifts of the heart	What positive qualities do people say you have?		
	Who are the people in your life that you give to?		
	How do you give to them?		
	When was the last time you shared with someone else? What was it?		
	What do you give that makes you feel good?		
	What do you hope to achieve		
Gifts of the hands	What do you enjoy doing?		
	What do people say you are good at?		
	What do you find easy?		

We suggest you build a directory of who your community members are and what they are bringing to the community, the 'head, heart and hands' that all community members can have access to, both their own and that of others.

You can also add in new questions or vary them to help people identify what they would like to learn and how they would like to develop by engaging with and being part of the workplace community.

Process – share the head, hearts and hands template with community members and ask them to complete it. Seek a couple of volunteers in the community to analyze, collate the responses and populate the members' directory. Feed this back to the community to stimulate discussion. Make the directory open and available to all community members.

Outcomes – community members have a rich understanding of what they and others bring to the community. An understanding of the richness of the life experience in the wider community and a general understanding of what others bring and are looking to do. A directory of community members and an understanding of what they bring to the work of the community in terms of skills and abilities and also in terms of attitudes and personality. When the workplace community comes to a close community members can review their head, heart and hands checklist to see what has changed and what new things being a community member has brought to them. What new things they have learnt about themselves and what new skills and abilities they have developed.

Next steps – keep access to the directory open and available for all members to browse. Use the head, heart and hands tool to help induct new members as they join. Encourage people to keep the directory alive by reviewing and updating.

The buy-in benchmark

Understanding contribution (Figure 7.1).

- **Bystanders** – that is people who understand the purpose, and process of the community but are not committed to it and are not involving themselves in it and most probably not even joined
- **Weak links** – these are people who have joined the community but have little contact with the community and have not done very much perhaps other than lurk. Most likely they do not understand what is expected of them and therefore do not understand what to do
- **Loose cannons** – these are people who are very committed but lack the understanding to make things happen in the way that will have most impact and make the most contribution
- **Champions** – understand, are committed and getting on with it

Purpose and use – to identify to what extent community members are contributing, in a positive way, to the workplace community and helping to enable it to fulfill its promise. To stimulate discussion about

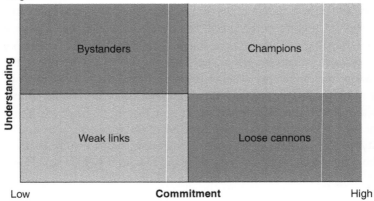

High

Understanding

Low   **Commitment**   High

Bystanders

Champions

Weak links

Loose cannons

FIG 7.1 / The buy-in benchmark

how people show and demonstrate buy-in to a workplace community way of working. What to do about those who become 'free riders' or start to exert a negative influence on the community and get in the way of its effective functioning.

We suggest that you use this tool to encourage people to reflect on their participation and help them keep focused and committed to the scope, theme and purpose of the community. You can also use this to help assess how much people have bought into the idea of workplace community ways of working, based upon their level of understanding and their commitment to this new way of working.

Process – share the template with people and ask them to mark on it where they think they are and where they think other community members are. Analyze the results. If you have mostly champions then job done! Feed this back to your community members and congratulate them and yourself! If, as is more likely, you have a spread of responses then ask yourself and community members the following questions:

If people have scored low on the understanding dimension:

• Have we all done enough work to help people understand how workplace communities work?

- Do we feel we have communicated the role, purpose, theme and scope of the workplace community clearly enough? Do people understand what we are all about? Review your induction plan. Check to see if there are things you need to add to it and whether there are induction processes you need to repeat to get people on board.
- Are our tools and technology fit for purpose? Or are they too difficult or overly complex for people to engage with? Are they becoming a disabler rather than a community enabler?

If people have scored low on the commitment scale then:

- Revisit your mini social network analysis and double check that you have connected with the right people. Do they really have an interest in the topic? Or have they joined for some other reason?
- Review your stakeholder engagement plan – does this give you any clues as to what might be going on and why people lack engagement?
- Connect with your OD practitioner and explore with them how to identify if what you are experiencing is an unwillingness to commit or is it that people don't know how to commit?
- Test out your findings with community members – we suggest you pick two or three to have a discussion with to validate and develop your thoughts and ideas before sharing this with the wider community.

In addition it may also be helpful to use the buy-in benchmark to keep track of the levels of commitment and understanding of your stakeholders.

Outcomes – a shared understanding of the balance between commitment and understanding in your community and a plan as to what to do about it.

Next steps – either keep on doing what you are doing because it is working, or lead a community refresh. That is a re-induction and a re-statement of the community's purpose, scope and theme. You may also need to invite more members to refresh the community. Develop a plan for challenging community members about why they are not engaging or contributing.

Sense of community index

How do people feel about being a community member? (Table 7.6).

Purpose and use – to understand the extent to which members of your community actually feel they are part of the community. This tool will help you and community members understand how engaged they are in the processes of the workplace community. This can be used as a follow up to the buy-in benchmark and will help you identify other issues you may need to address to ensure the community's health and make it the kind of place where people do great work.

Process – share the tool and analyze the results

Outcomes – an understanding of the overall health of your community and the identification of possible issues. So, for example, if community members score low on 'Q10 – it is very important to me to be a part of

Table 7.6   Sense of community index

Question		True/False	Comments
I think the [Community name] is a good place for me to be.			
People in this community share the same values.			
Other community members and I want the same things from the community.			
I can recognize most of the people who are in this community			
I feel I belong in this community.			
Very few community members know me.			
I care about what other community members think of my actions.			
I have no influence over what this community is like.			
If there is a problem in this community members can get it solved.			
It is very important to me to be part of this community.			
People in this community generally don't get along with each other.			
I expect to be in this community for a long time.			

this community' then you need to think through how this is likely to impact on the work of the community and develop actions, using the tools in this section, to address it.

Next steps – a revised plan, with identified actions, for community development to be shared with community members. Identified roles to help support the plan and keep track of the workplace community's development.

The cult checklist

Checking to see if your workplace community has started to exhibit cult-like behavior? (Table 7.7).

Purpose and use – this checklist will help you to determine the extent to which your community is showing signs of moving from being a healthy workplace community to a cult. By cult, in this context, we mean a closed and self-explaining system. If your workplace community is beginning to turn cult-like the only reference points it will use and choose to believe are those from within the community. It will at best distrust and at worst completely lose any connection with the wider organization. By doing so it creates its own set of beliefs that are not tested in or validated by the wider world. The only truth the community holds dear to is the truth it generates for itself.

All challenges to this are strongly resisted. If people, either inside or outside the workplace community, challenge these beliefs then they are usually accused of not believing enough and ultimately will be excluded. Schisms will start to emerge. Maintaining the workplace community as a closed self-explaining system becomes more important than any work the community needs to do. Signs that this might be happening to your community include:

- An over-focus on a leader (this may or may not be you!) who is seen as all-knowing and all-powerful
- Unquestioning commitment and no challenge, supportive or otherwise to issues and ideas. Those who do raise any challenges get

Table 7.7   The cult checklist

The community is:	True/False	Comments
Focused on a leader and displays excessively zealous, unquestioning commitment.		
Preoccupied with making money as opposed to a balance between achievement and doing the best work of our lives		
Elitist, claiming a special, exalted status for itself. Its leader(s), and members feel they have a special mission to save the company		
Questioning, doubt, and dissent are discouraged or even punished		
Mind-numbing techniques such as debilitating work routines are used to suppress doubts		
Leadership dictates sometimes in great detail how members should feel, think, act and behave		
The community has a polarized us-versus-them mentality the them being the wider organization		
The community teaches or implies that its exalted ends justify its means		
Leadership induces guilt feelings in members to control them		
Community members' subservence to the group causes them to give up personal goals and activities		
Community members are expected to devote inordinate amounts of time to the community		

excluded. They are considered as bad and not worthy of engaging with. They may be encouraged to leave the community or simply not invited to engage with any community activities to which they could make a legitimate and constructive contribution

- A sense of community elitism. The workplace community has an exalted sense of its self, members and leaders. Members feel they have a special mission to save the organization. Only they can do this. All alternate views are rejected.

You may also need help from an OD specialist to help you work this through and sort it out.

Outcomes – an understanding of whether your workplace community has become, or is moving towards becoming, a cult and an action plan either to make sure this does not happen or to deal with it if it is happening.

Next steps – these can include having one-on-one discussions with key community members who are at the heart of this. These can be extremely difficult conversations and we would strongly recommend that you rehearse them with your friendly OD practitioner. You may also want to involve other key stakeholders and invite them into the community to add new challenges. You can also keep reminding community members of the purpose, scope and theme of the community. If the cult has become so entrenched then you may need to consider closing the community and starting again.

From subject to citizen

Finding out what belonging means to community members. A milder form of a cult is where the workplace community becomes 'the court of the king or queen'. People start to feel as if they are subjects of the community rather than empowered citizens of it with a sense of shared ownership and belonging. The king or queen can be a person such as the leader of the community, a key stakeholder or even the wider organization itself. (Table 7.8).

Purpose and use

Use this tool to help you and other community members identify the degree to which community members feel they are citizens or subjects of the community. As subjects, creativity is more limited and bounded by expectations, whereas citizens feel more able to assert themselves, have a greater sense of personal responsibility and access to all of their personal resources. Nothing is out of bounds or proscribed.

Process – share the inventory with the community, collate and feedback the results. Engage in a discussion on the findings with the community

Table 7.8   From subject to citizen

Subject	Score (1–5)	Citizen	Score (1–5)
Privileges		Rights	
Subject to authority		The individual is sovereign	
Potential domination		Choice to exit	
Little real say in how treated in or what happens		A right to be heard	
Does as they are told		Distributed power	
Power closely held and focused		Meaning made in many places, post-modern	
Only one or two ways of understanding		Leaders have clear duties to the people	
Members are subject to leadership		Rights and responsibilities	
Treason		Open and individually focused	
Leadership or institutionally centered		Space for individual, collective participation	
Agenda set top down and managed		Choice and freedom	
Feudalism		Individuals feeling free to articulate their needs, wants and offers	
One way chain of command		Authenticity, knowledge and empowerment	
Disengaged populace		Shared satisfaction	
De-personalized consumers		Independent actors	
Blind compliance, do nothing, do as your told		Freedom of action	

and develop actions to shift and maintain the balance towards a citizen enabled workplace community.

Next steps – you may need to challenge those people who are adopting a queen bee approach. Be aware that this may be unconscious on their part. It may not have anything to do with their conscious exercise of power and influence. In many cases it is simply a result of people exercising the leadership position and role they have in the wider organization. They don't fully understand that the workplace community is a different place where leadership and management are handled very differently. Ask yourself, have you inducted these people appropriately and helped them understand what they are joining and how best to share and manage the fluidity of power?

After action review

This will help you understand what happened – what your workplace community achieved or failed to achieve (Table 7.9).

Purpose and use – to help people understand and make sense of their experience of being a member of a workplace community and contributing to its achievements. This is best used when the workplace community has moved into the Transformation stage and you need to decide if the work of the community is over and it is time to say goodbye and close or help it to transform into something else. The process will help community members make sense of their experience,

Table 7.9   After action review

Question	Expectation?	What happened?
What did we intend to achieve?		
What have we actually achieved? • What went well • What could have been better		
What have we learnt? • About the theme and issue • About workplace communities • About ourselves as community members and as employees of the wider organization • About the wider organization		
What would we do differently next time?		
What should we do now to enable the transformation of the community?		

learn from it and move on. It will also help the wider organization to understand what the experience has meant to community members and to learn what worked, what did not work and what to do differently next time.

Process – share the after action review template with community members and ask them to complete it. Make space in the community for people to share their experiences. Gather the lessons learned and publish.

Outcomes – a set of lessons learned for individual community members and for the wider organization. A sense of impending closure on the part of community members, it's coming to an end. A validation of their experience and public recognition of what being part of the workplace community has meant to them.

Next steps – share the lessons learned inside and outside of the workplace community. Get recognition for what the workplace community has achieved and how they achieved it. Invite key stakeholders to give and share their reaction to the work of the community, both inside and outside of the community. Find ways to ensure that the work of the community and its members is appropriately recognized and rewarded.

A variation – headlines and highlights

Ask people to submit tabloid newspaper-style headlines that highlight the achievements of the community. They can submit more than one and encourage them to focus on the good, the bad and the ugly!

You can also encourage them to submit a second set of headlines that capture the personal highlights of the experience for them. What they have learned and what they will take away from the process, what worked for them and what didn't.

Purpose and use – you may also choose to use the headlines and highlights tool as a quick and dirty variation on the after action review theme. We would suggest you use this in situations where your workplace community has had a short life or for some unforeseen reason has had to close sooner than you anticipated.

The outcomes and next steps are similar to those expected from the after action review tool.

Risk mapping and management

Risk sssesment – understanding the risks your community may face and how these might be mitigated (Figure 7.2)

Risk mapping matrix

Risk mitigation

Purpose and use – this tool will help you to identify and manage potential risks to your community and help you head them off at the pass! We suggest you use this tool as you start planning (Table 7.10).

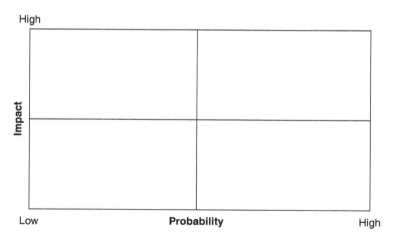

FIG 7.2 Risk mapping and management

Table 7.10   Risk mitigation

Issue	Action	Responsible	

Process – on your own or with others brainstorm the kinds of risks you think your workplace community may be subject to. Once you have a list, plot them on the matrix placing them in terms of probability – that is how likely is this risk to occur – and impact that is how high or low the impact would be on your plans if this risk actually occurred.

Some risks may be very unlikely but if they do occur they could have a highly negative impact on the workplace community and totally destroy what you are trying to achieve. Other risks may be very likely to happen but have little or no discernable impact. Once you have mapped your risks use the mitigation table to develop actions to help manage the risks. We suggest you prioritize and work on those actions that have a high probability of occurring and potentially a high negative impact on the community.

Share you risk map and mitigating actions with community members and ask them to contribute their own risks and mitigation actions. It is also a good idea to share this with your stakeholders and supporters like your tame IT specialist and friendly OD practitioner. This is for two reasons: firstly they may be able to come up with risks and mitigating actions you have not thought of and secondly if they are forewarned then when you ask for help at some point in the future they will also be forearmed.

Outcomes – an agreed and shared risk map and associated mitigation actions to help you manage identified risks. We advise you to review this regularly with community members and by doing so ensure that there are no nasty surprises!

8

Rewards and Benefits

What's in it for you, me and them?

In this chapter we will explore the benefits of a community way of working and the rewards it can bring. We will look at this from the perspective of you as the community initiator and from the standpoint of community members. And finally we will consider what the wider organization can gain by supporting an initiative to launch workplace communities.

There are many ways in which a community will be of benefit to the wider organization, as well as to its members. Value will be created in both the short and long term. In general, short-term value to the organization will be related to improving business outcomes, in the long term the value will be related to the development of organizational capabilities.

For the individual the benefits in the short term will generally be related to improving their experience of work and in the longer term to fostering their professional development.

There are very strong links between what we cover in this chapter and the Chapter Measurement and Meaning. The latter provides you with ways of tracking and measuring outcomes, rewards and benefits. In this chapter the focus is more on the personal and developmental benefits/rewards and less on business outcomes.

We will also look at the opposite or shadow side of benefits and rewards. The shadow side involves the risks you and others might personally be running and the negative consequences you and others may experience as a result of launching or engaging with a workplace community. None of this is to put you off initiating a workplace community. It is more a case of forewarned is forearmed.

It should be noted that the benefits of a workplace community, even the short term benefits, will not be achieved until the community has reached a certain level of maturity, and this will take time and effort, but once achieved will be more than worth the investment.

Definitions

Before we get started we need to be clear on a few definitions so that we can be sure that we are thinking in the same way. Reward and benefit are not synonymous, so lets start with a definition or two. The *Oxford English Dictionary* defines a benefit as:

> An advantage or profit gained from something

And a reward as being:

> a gift of something to someone in recognition of their service, efforts or achievement

As an employee your rewards include your salary, and any bonuses you receive for your efforts. Your benefits will range from a pension scheme through to health care and a company car. There is also another level of benefits that you receive, depending on who you work for, the prestige of being employed by such a glorious organization!

Another example which may help clarify the difference between the two and which is perhaps more closely related to workplace communities is as follows: You post regularly on a social media website. The reward for your post may be when someone 'likes' one of your posts, makes a positive comment or moves you to the top of a leader board. The benefit you accrue for your activity is that people start to recognize that you have skills, capabilities and knowledge in a certain area; your reputation. This in turn may lead to you being invited to contribute to other exciting initiatives and to you becoming recognized as a thought leader.

Motivation

At the heart of any exploration of rewards and benefits sits the issue of personal motivation. Motivation is generally divided into two categories, intrinsic and extrinsic.

Extrinsic motivation is when we do something to be rewarded or to avoid something bad. The motivation to do it comes from outside of oneself and represents something you would like to acquire or avoid. Examples of what you might like to acquire include monetary-based rewards such as cash, vouchers for goods, status symbols like expensive cars or clothes, points and prizes and the top position on a leader board. Examples of things you would like to avoid include losing, shame, ignominy, pain, being left out, ignored and so on. So, for example, you may choose to join a workplace community to be recognized and noticed, to have people 'like' your contributions. To feel valued for what you bring to the community and acknowledged for your contributions.

Intrinsic motivation is when we do something because the very act of doing it is rewarding in and of itself. We are internally driven to do it. Our passion for learning and our love of our trade or craft are sufficient to keep us motivated and engaged. Somehow we cannot stop ourselves from getting involved. So, for example, you may join a workplace community because of your passion for the issue and topic it is addressing. You can think of nothing better than having the opportunity to share your passion with other like-minded individuals. Leader boards, points and prizes are either of no interest or purely incidental to your participation.

In our opinion neither kind of motivation is better than the other. They are morally neutral per se. It is only when we see them in action and look at the consequences that we can make a judgment as to their impact and whether it is good or bad, helpful or unhelpful.

If people in a workplace community are strongly driven extrinsically then they may only be interested in the rewards and go for these at any cost. We worked with one community that decided to use points and prizes to drive participation. This was a community of over 2,000 members. The organization was going through a lot of change and community members knew that redundancies were on the cards. A number of senior decision-makers were community members. A lot of community members felt that if they were seen to be at the top or high up the community's leader board they would be seen to be vital and popular members of the community and this might help them keep their jobs. When we started to examine the nature of the contributions we found that people were contributing everything from film reviews to where to eat and drink in New York! Very few of the contributions had anything to do with the issue.

Likewise if people are only intrinsically motivated then you may find that participation becomes erratic with people only contributing to the specific area they are interested in and not thinking more broadly about the whole. For example your community may be focused on sales and marketing in South America. Your organization is keen to develop an overall marketing plan for your products and services for the whole of the region. You have initiated a global workplace community to help with this. You believe there are lessons to be learned from other parts of the world. For instance you know that South East Asia has a great, holistic plan for sales and marketing that has been very successful. You launch your workplace community but find that very few people from South East Asia join. In addition you find that people from Latin America are only interested in their specific country and are not viewing the region as whole. Community members are only driven by intrinsic motivation.

In both examples the community initiators got the balance wrong between intrinsic and extrinsic motivation. When you are thinking about launching a workplace community you need to consider this very carefully. You may also need to change and shift your motivation strategy as the community moves forward and starts to evolve through the different stages we described in Chapter 5.

Generosity

Healthy and successful workplace communities are driven by generosity. One person's desire to make a contribution to the whole. When we have explored this with people what we have found at the heart of their generosity is a belief that if they are generous and share then others will also share and be generous. This mirrors the research of Richard Titmus, a nineteenth century British social researcher, who coined the term 'the gift relationship' (Titmus, 1970).

Titmus carried out research into blood donations in a number of countries exploring what motivated people to donate. In some countries people were paid to donate blood and in others they gave it for free. He found that in those countries where people were paid there was a large amount of wastage of blood, often shortages, and the quality of the blood was very variable, with more incidences of hepatitis, a killer in the 1950s and 1960s. So paying people resulted in worse blood being collected than in those countries where no payment was made. He coined the term 'the gift relationship to describe why this was the case. He believed his findings showed that people are far more altruistic than we give them credit for. By placing a blood donation in a blood bank people felt they were storing something for the future. If they give to people in a time of need, then others would give to them at their time of need.

We believe this to be at the heart of a successfully functioning workplace community. In essence you are asking people to give the gift of their time, experience, thinking and creativity with the expectation that others will do the same. Altruism and the gift relationship are hard to measure however you will know when they are in place and functioning!

Gamification

Gamification is something relatively new in the workplace. By gamification we mean the translation of the kinds of thinking and processes that drive on-line gaming and the application of this to the workplace. Gamification taps into people's competitive natures and their desires to win. In on-line games people are rewarded for their success by receiving points, badges to mark their achievement, the unlocking of another level of the game and so on. Players' achievements are then highlighted on a leader board for all to see. The nearer you are to the top, the more successful you are. You will already no doubt see a link between the paragraphs above about extrinsic motivation and the idea of gamification.

Increasingly gamification is being used in the workplace to engage both employees and customers. We know of examples where employees are encouraged to comment on news posts on a company intranet by being given points and badges for the number of comments they make. We also know of a company that wanted to increase feedback and generosity and encouraged employees to award virtual 'kudos badges' to people they felt had gone over and above what was expected of them in their role.

We also know of examples where companies have used gamification to help customers understand their products and services. One example is the 'My Starbucks Reward Program', an app with different levels of loyalty rewards. Scientists and academics have been using gamification to drive their initiatives forward. Some examples are 'Phylo' a puzzle game contributing to genetic disease research and 'Foldit' helping find cures for HIV/AIDS. These are often called 'games with purpose' or 'purposeful play'.

Gamification can play a useful part in a workplace community. You may want to consider whether it is something that will help encourage engagement and participation. Bear in mind though the above story about the community where people got so obsessed with being at the top of the leader board that they forgot, or chose to ignore, what the workplace community had been set up for. People can become more interested in playing the game than the issue in hand.

What's in it for me, you and them?

Here we will explore in more detail what you, community members and the wider organization can expect in terms of rewards and benefits related to motivation. We will look at the risks associated with motivation. By no means are the lists exhaustive and we would encourage you to add to them so that they reflect more clearly the culture of your organization and the nature of the workplace community you wish to initiate.

What's in it for you?

As the workplace community initiator you need to ask yourself the following questions to explore your personal motivation and also your expectations of rewards and benefits for your efforts:

- What is important to you personally about launching a workplace community?
- What do you personally hope to achieve?
- What will keep you going if and when times get tough?

Let's look at some of the things that might motivate and demotivate you, the benefits and rewards you might realize along with the potential perils (Table 8.1).

What's in it for me?

As someone who has been invited to join a workplace community you need to ask yourself the following questions:

- What do I hope to achieve?
- What will keep me involved and contributing?
- How will I manage my time and do I have enough?
- What level of involvement do I want to have?
- What do I expect to give and receive?

Lets look at some things that might be motivating you and the benefits and rewards you might realize along with the potential perils as well (Table 8.2).

What's in it for them?

As a senior leader or manager in an organization and who has been approached about sponsoring or giving your blessing to the setting

Table 8.1   What's in it for you – benefits matrix

Motivation	Benefit	Reward	Risk	
Solving a problem	Recognition of achievement both within the community and by the wider organization	Connection to senior leaders, exposure higher up in the organization	You may uncover a hornets nest!' The problem may not be solvable and may be a dilemma You cannot deliver on the plausible promise to community members or the wider organization	
Exploring an opportunity	Having identified something Making something manageable and doable	Getting clarity and having others recognize this Being seen as brave and courageous Harvesting diverse ideas that makes you wiser	Paralysis by analysis You don't get sufficient diversity to explore opportunities in a holistic way	
Raising engagement	Being recognized as contributing to the health of the organization, its well-being and agility Being recognized as helping to keep talented employees with the company	Being invited to contribute to other issues, finding out more Being known and rewarded as an engaging leader, someone who brings out discretionary effort and high performance	People may get disheartened and start to feel the organization is not as good as they thought it was! A few critical voices, especially of opinion leaders, can ruin engagement and energy	
Being noticed	Being seen as having more skills and capabilities than people thought	Changing your position on the organization's talent map. Being seen as a valuable resource that must be kept!	You may get noticed for the wrong things! Your self-image may be challenged and you may get feedback you don't want or expect.	

up of a workplace community you need to ask yourself the following questions:

• Do I understand what this is all about?
• What do I need to know to feel comfortable in supporting this?

Table 8.2   What's in it for me – benefits matrix

Motivation	Benefit	Reward	Risk
Being involved and not being left out	You get noticed, your voice is heard Feelings of belonging and contribution	Your talent is recognized and you get considered for other roles	You may have nothing to contribute and people wonder why you are there
Getting the answer to questions and solutions to problems	It makes your work easier You learn different ways of probing into an area, prioritizing, and getting solutions	You can be seen as a problem solver and facilitator of learning	There may not be an answer People may not be as committed to the inquiry as you are and not focus on what you want to
Meeting new people	You expand your network	You meet people who may be useful in the future	It depends on who joins
Finding new opportunities	Your find out your skills are transferable to other areas in the organization	A new job opportunity emerges	You realise your are trapped in your current role
Getting noticed	You become recognized as a thought leader	Your skills are recognized by others and your position in the talent pipeline moves in a positive way	People find out you don't know as much as they thought you did.

- How much do I personally want to get involved?
- What metrics can I use to help me understand both what is going on and how to measure the outcomes?
- Can I get my manager's support and the organization's commitment to spend time and resources on this? (Table 8.3)

Final thoughts and conclusion

Remember, you can encourage and stimulate people's motivation but you cannot create it or mandate it. The most motivated people in

Table 8.3   What's in it for them – benefits matrix

Motivation	Benefit	Reward	Risk
Tapping into collective intelligence	You find the wisdom of the crowd	You get answers and solutions you never could have dreamed of	You find there isn't as much intelligence as you hoped
People seeing the organization in the round	Employees start to feel a much greater sense of ownership for the whole of the organization rather than just their part of it	People start making decisions that benefit the whole e.g. more care over expenses, tighter management of budgets	People don't like what they find out about the whole and retreat into their part of it
Focused work and effort	People are focusing on what matters and getting things done	You resolve long-standing issues and irritations in the organization in a systematic way	People are over-focused to the exclusion of what else needs to be done to ensure success
Strategy fulfillment	The business strategy is really being worked on and things are getting done	Business outcomes and measurable success in such things as sales and product development etc.	People criticize the strategy and spend time proving why it won't work. The strategy gets ridiculed
Greater employee engagement and commitment	People feel part of something and this spills over into their everyday activities – generosity is contagious	People are using more discretionary effort and getting things done faster, and this reduces overall costs	Employees may drift and become engaged with things you don't want them to be engaged with…
Unleashing creativity	Employees tap into latent skills and creativity and apply this with enthusiasm and excitement	Creativity leads to business improvements, cost savings, new products and ideas	People may choose to apply their creativity to issues that you do not support but that are of interest to them

(Continued)

Table 8.3   Continued

Motivation	Benefit	Reward	Risk
Being seen as a forward-thinking organization	You enhance your reputation as a twenty-first century organization being seen as a center of creativity and innovation	It is easier and cheaper to recruit people. Retention is not a problem Organization flexibility has increased	You can be seen as being faddy and unfocussed just interested in the latest 'whizzy' idea.
Enhanced capacity and capabilities	Your employees learn news skills and develop their capabilities	This is a very cost-efficient way to develop people as it is self-managed and self-directed	People may learn things you don't want or need them to bother with

the world can become frustrated and discouraged from time to time. Community members need to have ways of seeking and expressing appreciation. What you can do is to make sure you think through the issues of motivation, rewards and benefits as you initiate the community and keep an eye on this as your community grows, develops and evolves.

A simple process is to pick the benefits, rewards and risks that apply specifically to your scenario and then monitor if and how they materialize. Our Chapter, Measurement and Meaning will help highlight progress and degree of success. You must make sure to communicate progress and any setbacks, celebrate success, and ask community members to help rectify any derailing.

Acting as a role model, openly sharing your expectations on benefits and rewards, and encouraging everyone to express and harvest them, will make motivation authentic and keep the community culture resilient and positive.

9

Measurement and Meaning

Introduction

In this chapter we will help you develop a framework for measuring the effectiveness of your workplace community at its different stages, from Initiation through to Transformation. We will provide you with a number of very practical measures that you can tailor to the theme, scope and purpose of your workplace community and then use to create your own measures and metrics. In addition we will help you think through which measures to include in your community scorecard. These will be of particular use to you, community members and stakeholders to understand the current stage, activity and contribution of the workplace community.

We suggest that you select the key measures that are most appropriate to your workplace community; you may also choose to segment some of the measures to reflect areas of particular interest or particular groups of members.

An obsession with measuring?

In today's organizations being able to develop clear and focused outcomes, measure them and adjust your processes accordingly to make sure you meet your target, is key to being recognized, as doing something that is successful and worthwhile. The market and shareholders are all used to being fed performance data and to using it as a way to judge whether an organization is being successful or not. This used to be pretty much the preserve of the private sector, however, in the last 15 years or so the culture of measurement has spread across all sectors. Some would argue that we have become obsessed with measurement to the point where the search for the holy grail of metrics is driving out actual performance along with creativity and innovation.

We will all of us have heard the quote 'You can't manage what you can't measure', attributed to W. Edward Deming. Most of today's organizations live by this mantra. The truth is that this has wrongly entered organization folklore as a rule to manage and live by. Deming actually stated that one of the seven deadly diseases of management is running a company on visible figures alone! It is worth holding this in mind as you move through this chapter. Many of today's organizations have an unhealthy relationship to measurement and metrics. They spend a lot of time and money on developing metrics, buying systems and setting up processes that will track and measure them, as opposed to actually understanding what needs to be in place to allow for excellent performance and to develop the kind of workplaces where people feel able to give of their best.

Of course you will need to find ways to demonstrate that your workplace community represents value for money and is worth the energy and effort involved. You also need a set of measures that help you understand what is happening. Your stakeholders will need to feel assured that the time and effort people are spending on workplace community activities are likely to make a contribution to the overall success of the wider organization. They need to feel and know that you will be adding value and not just wasting time and creating a distraction from what really needs to be done. To reassure them, you need to be able to speak their language. Most likely this will be the language of metrics and measurement. So it is important that you develop measures, within the context of workplace community ways of working, that make sense to your stakeholders, measures that they can understand and that they can relate to.

Metrics as an enabler

It is important to see metrics as an enabler and not as a turgid task. Something you have to do to feed the beast. At the same time it is equally important not to become so obsessed by them that you lose focus on other equally important tasks and activities as you initiate and launch your workplace community.

Remember that workplace communities are a collaborative affair. You may have to take the initial responsibility for establishing a measurement framework but once you have an outline, remember to tap into the collective intelligence of the community to help you develop it further and populate it. Getting the workplace community's engagement around measurement is vital. You will need them to provide data as well as help you interpret different measures. They will also need to use the community's metrics dashboard and balanced scorecard to connect with their stakeholders, helping them understand the valuable contribution the workplace community is making to the wider organization and their own contribution to it.

Measuring success

Measuring success and setting targets is critical. Not just in terms of helping community members to understand what is happening, in a very practical way, but also to help you manage the expectations of the wider organization. It is one of the key ways of making sure your community remains connected to the 'real world' and does not get lost in its own world.

So you have decided to explore setting up a workplace community as you feel that the issues you are facing would be better suited to collective intelligence rather than being managed and worked on in a more traditional manner. You believe the benefits will outweigh the effort it will take to establish a workplace community and work in this way. You have established a purpose, scope and theme and also feel the subject matter contains enough plausible promise and a clear bargain for those who may wish to join. You are planning to meet a number of key stakeholders and you know they will be interested and most likely supportive. However, you also know that they have very traditional views about work and the way things should be done. You also know that even though every bone in your body is telling you a workplace community is the right way forward this intuition will not be enough to convince them to positively support at best or benignly forbear to interfere at worst. You know that especially if you are going to ask for a budget you will need more than just a good story. What you need are some compelling metrics! You need numbers and credible ways of measuring success at regular intervals that you can share with your stakeholders to show how things are on track and that the community is doing what it needs to do. You know that they will be interested in is having a clear return on investment. Not just for the time, energy and effort it will take you and others to get the community going but also on the end result. How will you know if the effort was worth it and the community is working?

Challenges

Workplace communities are new and unusual and we are only beginning to learn and understand how they operate and function effectively. Traditional organizations have a long and varied history of being able to track and measure their performance and effectiveness. We are only at the beginning of this journey for workplace communities; we are just starting to understand the patterns of interaction and contribution that ultimately make a workplace community work, and this includes developing the best way to identify and measure their success. When thinking about the effectiveness of workplace communities as opposed to traditional organizations we face the following challenges:

- Workplace communities are all about voluntary effort and commitment and not about mandated action. As we have explored earlier, you cannot force people to be a member of a community -- they have to want to join, the community needs both plausible promise and a 'bargain'. If you do force people to become members, or even 'force' contribution, it is unlikely that this contribution will deliver the value expected.
- The community is driven by the interest and generosity of it members, not by fixed tasks and targets.
- In traditional organizations, roles are fixed and bounded by job descriptions. In the workplace community roles are transient and negotiable.
- Community members can choose to join a community and leave when they want to. They may choose to be active on issues that interest them and to simply lurk if they feel they have nothing to contribute. In the wider organization people do not have the same opportunities for choice and flexibility. They are expected to fulfill their job description and work towards agreed tasks and targets. They cannot choose to contribute one day and not the next.
- At times the community may need to be inwardly focused to manage its processes and this can look like self-indulgence and a waste of time to those on the outside. Traditional organizations strive to be more focused on the task and working to explicit plans with measurable contributions. They tend to be very action orientated with little truck for navel gazing.
- The measurement of communities will be influenced by the general climate in the organization. Community activities and members' contributions will be influenced by how they feel about the general organization.
- Communities take time to develop. There can be unrealistic expectations that the community will deliver to the wider organization before it has reached the stage where it is able to truly deliver.

So much of what appears to be going on in a workplace community can be considered to be 'soft stuff'. That is, it is about building relationships, unleashing creativity and stimulating cross-organizational collaboration. It is not all about the 'hard stuff', such as what measurable resources are being used to produce which outputs. In many organizations the soft stuff does not get much traction with only hard facts having currency. Ian explored this in a post titled 'Making the Soft Stuff Hard' in our joint blog 'The Illusion of Work', which you can find here: http://theillusionofwork.wordpress.com. This causes a number of dilemmas as soft stuff, and by that we mean generosity, friendship, trust, sense of belonging, comfort and feelings, is at the heart of what makes a workplace community the kind of place people want to be active in and contribute to. It is only when this soft stuff is in place that the community will start to function effectively and provide the opportunity for innovation and achievement. The example measures and processes we describe below cover measuring the hard stuff and also the soft stuff and explore how best to represent them both inside and outside the workplace community.

Here is an example. You can count the number of members of your community relatively easily and also the rate at which people choose to join. This will give you a good hard measure. It is important to know the size of your community and also the geographical and organizational spread. However what is more important is to be able to tell if you have the right members and to have measures in place that will help you to do this. Another example. You will want to know and measure the levels of activity amongst and between community members. Again this will be a very useful measure to help you understand the energy in the community. However if this is measured solely in terms of the number of posts and does not measure the nature or value of the posts then it is not much use. You may have a very large community of people who are extremely busy discussing the latest episode of their favorite soap opera rather than focusing on the purpose, theme and issue the community was set up to address.

All of this creates challenges when we come to measuring both what is happening in the community and how effective it is being. None of this should stop us from making the effort. We just need to be creative and look at things slightly differently.

Many of the community and collaboration tools used today will have built-in measurement and analytics capabilities. Review these capabilities with your tame IT support to determine which to use.

Categories of measurement

We have grouped measures into three categories: (1) those that measure the activity of the community, (2) those that measure the value within the community, and (3) those that measure the performance of the community in relation to the wider organization.

Here are some examples of measures in each of our categories:

- **Activity** – what is going on, what is happening within your community? Example measures in this category include:
  - Number of members, and types of member (visitors, novices, regulars, leaders, elders)
  - Number of new members,
  - Member activity, daily visits, length of stay
  - Number of new/active conversations
  - Depth/size/span of conversations,
  - Length of posts
  - Number questions asked/responses given
  - Speed of responsiveness
  - Number of contributions
  - **Internal community value** – the value created within the community and its members. Examples of measures in this category include:
  - Value of the community to its members
  - The usefulness of the community
  - The knowledge captured or created by the community
  - The level of support provided by the community
  - Learning and development as a result of community membership
  - Improved collaboration and cooperation

- How helpful the community is to its members
- Members' sense of belonging
- Levels of members' engagement
- **Community performance** – the value created by the community to the wider organization. These will typically be business or customer related measures and will be related to specific outcomes for your organization. Examples in this category include:
  - Number of customer problems solved
  - Reduced time to market of a product or service
  - Improved quality of product or service
  - Cost savings or cost avoidance
  - Improved innovation
  - Improved organizational ways of working
  - Increased engagement on the part of employees

Targets can be set for all categories. It is good practice to consider the measures and set targets at the outset of your community.

For online workplace communities measures in the activity category will typically come from the technology platform, and its reporting and/or analytics capabilities. The second category: internal community value will typically be captured and followed through community polls, surveys, and by interviewing community members. The third category: community performance is where to measure and track the ROI of the community and its value to the organization and it impact on the bottom line. All three categories are important both to the organization and to community members. However our experience has been that ROI is the one that your stakeholders and the wider organization is likely to be most interested in.

While some of the measures will be applicable across all stages of the community's life cycle; others will be more appropriate to a specific developmental stage.

We advise:

- When planning to launch your community and for engaging with stakeholders and potential community members, establish and agree the criteria for measuring your ROI. It is easier to set the criteria for this at the beginning and adjust as you go forward, as opposed to trying to establish this retrospectively and then look for measures and metrics that will fit. This will also help focus and clarify the purpose of the workplace community.

• Think about how your community will change, grow and evolve over time and at the various stages your community will go through from initiation through to transformation using the community evolution model. You can select the appropriate measures and set specific targets for each stage of your workplace community's development.

• When your workplace community finally comes to an end and you choose to close it, measuring the overall success and the ROI will allow members, past and present, to celebrate their contribution to the wider organization and share this with their stakeholders.

Scorecards

When approaching the issue of measuring we encourage you to be systematic and rigorous. We recommend choosing a number of measures and forming a scorecard. This scorecard can be used with the stakeholders, and also to reflect the health of the community back to its members.

We suggest a scorecard follow the same three categories:

1. Activity – what is going on/happening in the community
2. Internal community value – within the community
3. Community performance – the value created external to the community

Choose the most appropriate measures under each category. A visual display of the scorecard in the form of a dashboard will make the understanding and interpretation easier. Some of the measures will be point in time, others you will want to track over time to see trends.

Using the tool or technology platform to provide a rich set of data, reports and analytics will significantly ease the human effort required, especially in the collection and processing of key metrics.

Return on investment

As previously mentioned we suggest that as part of your initial planning and prior to initiation and launch, you set some parameters in terms of the overall return on investment (ROI) of your workplace community. This will help to focus the purpose of the community and will make the 'plausible promise' more concrete in terms of expected targets and returns. You can then use this with stakeholders as well as community members to level set expectations and keep ideas about time, effort and measurement in people's minds. It will also help you engage with stakeholders and we suggest you encourage them to contribute to this process. In addition you can include your ROI plan as part of the induction process for new community members; again this will help with on-boarding and to bring clarity on the purpose of the community.

Developing your ROI plan

We have found the following questions very useful in helping us to develop an ROI plan. Ask yourself:

- What do I wish to achieve with this workplace community?
- What do I hope the wider organization will achieve by launching a workplace community?
- How important, at this time, are the theme, focus and issue for me?
- How important, at this time, are the theme, focus and issue for the wider organization?
- Will anyone notice if I do nothing and don't launch a workplace community?
- How will I evaluate the impact and outcome of the workplace community? What criteria will I use? What data will I need to support this? How will I gather this data? Who can help?
- How does the time effort, energy and resources I will need to launch my workplace community rank against other, competing, organizational issues?
- People only have so much discretionary energy they can give. How can I help them see that the workplace community you are proposing is the best way of using this?

If you work very carefully through these questions you will find it relatively easy to develop a return on investment plan with associated metrics and an idea of targets. You can then re-craft and re-shape this in conjunction with your stakeholders and potential community members (Table 9.1).

Measuring the process

In Chapter 6 'Stages of Community Development' we shared with you a model we have developed to track the stages your workplace community will move through as it matures and develops. We will now use this model and map onto it ways of measuring what is happening at each stage.

Planning prior to launch

During this stage develop your ROI plan and share this with key stakeholders and others who are willing to support you. You need to test it to make sure that it makes sense, that it will be easy to use and is worthwhile. Think about the potential membership, and activity levels that will be needed to achieve the ROI in your plan.

At this stage you should also have a chat with your tame IT specialist and ask them about the reporting and analytics functionality included

Table 9.1   ROI questions

Summary ROI question		Your answer	How you will measure
What I wish to achieve?			
What does the organization wish to achieve?			
Importance to me?			
Importance to the organization?			
If we do nothing?			
How to evaluate impact and outcomes?			
Ranking the community versus other issues			
Discretionary energy rating			

See: Return on investment (ROI) plan example at the end of this chapter.

in the tools you have chosen to use. It may well be that the reporting and analytic capabilities are only available to a 'super user' or system administrator. Before developing anything review these capabilities and determine if their ability to generate and capture metrics is sufficient.

It is usually straightforward to measure user activity; number of members, active members, members status (novice through to elder), members activity, number of conversations, depth of conversations, responsiveness, and so on. However it will usually require more specialized tools to carry out analysis on the content of the interactions for example sentiment analysis. Again there maybe tools within your organizations that are already being used for this purpose. It is worth checking to see if the customer-facing, or social media or digital marketing departments are using any such tool to interpret customer and consumer feedback.

Think through how you are going to track progress and what you need to do to support knowledge management and capturing outputs and outcomes. Again your IT specialist can help you with this. Your OD practitioner should also be able to help you develop a context-appropriate framework for tracking outputs and exploring outcomes. They should also be able to help you think through processes for knowledge management and data interrogation.

Measuring each stage

We believe that there is a set of baseline measures that can be used consistently throughout the workplace community life cycle. In addition we recommend a set of metrics and measurements for the individual stages of your community. We do not suggest that you use all of them or all of them all of the time. You are also not tied to just these metrics. Feel free to pick and choose and also, of course, to develop your own measures or variations of the measures we suggest. Although we have placed the metrics against the stages, as you will see the baseline measures are applicable during many of the stages.

When reading through this next section, remember the metaphor of the gardener in Chapter 4 Getting Started. No plant will grow well if you are constantly pulling it out of the soil to see how the roots are growing – so too with your workplace community. You need to ensure that your measurement strategy is an enabling one, rather than something that gets in the way and stops the workplace community getting on with its primary work. Yes measurement is important, in terms of working out what is going on and also to identify if things are not working. However, unless your community's scope, purpose and theme is about measurement it should not be allowed to dominate!

While the tools may enable you to poll and survey the community members whenever you wish, avoid the temptation to over-use this, especially where the results of any poll or survey are either not shared with the community, or are perceived as being of little value. You may want to know what the members think of the workplace community every day, but community members may not want to tell you every day! They are probably much more interested in getting on with the task in hand. Use non-intrusive (meaning you don't need to disturb the members of your community) measures as you wish, but take care when and how you use more intrusive data collection.

Focus on the stages

During each stage we will look at our three measurement categories:

1. **Activity** – what is going on/happening in the community (feel good measures)
2. **Internal community value** – within the community (feel connected measures)
3. **Community performance** – the value created for the wider organization (feel valued measures)

Stage 1 – initiation

The metrics at this stage are all about the initial buzz you are able to generate and that you personally experience. The focus here is on garnering interest and getting the right people to join. It is also about setting things in place from a metrics point of view. It will also be the starting point from which to track trends over time.

At this stage do not worry too much about the quality of the dialogue and processes of inquiry but rather think more about the nature of it. What is attracting people's attention and is a focus beginning to emerge? Visitors and the conversion of visitors to members will reflect the level of interest and intent (Table 9.2).

Table 9.2   Stage 1 – initiation: measurements

Category	Measure	Set a target	Measuring & reporting
Activity	Visitors	The number of people who are visitors (not registered members) to the community tool	Count Count per day Count per week Count per month Unique visit versus total visit count
	Members	The number people who join the community	Count Count per day Count per week Count per month Count per geography Count per business unit Count pre/post launch
	Member activity	Number of active members The frequency of visits and the time spent on each visit	Count of active members Number member visits per day Average time spent on each visit
	Conversations	Number of conversations started. Depth of conversation/threads Length of posts Contributions	Count of new conversation/ threads. (later on, per day, week or month) Count of the number of posts within a thread or conversation (by unique users versus repetitive posts by same members) Word count Contribution per members Age of conversations

(continued)

Table 9.2   Continued

Category	Measure	Set a target	Measuring & reporting
	Responsiveness	The speed with which posts and/ or questions are responded to	Average time of a response
Internal Community Value	Interest	The number of people who seek information about the community	Count
	Quality of Dialog	Number of sentences in a message, Number of responses in a thread Number of new ideas	Randomized count
	Was the launch successful	Good, bad, more work needed, number of people participated and number who provided suggestions	Poll and review of narrative comments
	Engagement and exploration	How many questions have been asked? Have members invited others to join?	Count
Community Performance	Interest	Are people talking about the community in the wider organization? Have people heard about it?	Ask and record Narrative comments Run a poll on the company's intranet home page asking if people have heard of the community

Stage 2 – potential

During the Potential stage we suggest you share your ROI and measurement framework with your community members. Have them contribute to the structure of it and also to start to populate it. Have them focus on what success looks like to them and help them capture this and provide them with ways of tracking it. This can be a fruitful community exercise.

Typically at this stage, visitor and member numbers will remain low; after all you have not launched the community yet! You may see regular contribution from initial key contributors, the potential nucleus of the community and they may be having some very in-depth dialog. In line with the number of members, the number of conversations or threads will be limited (Table 9.3).

Table 9.3   Stage 2 – potential: measurements

Category	Measure	Set a target	Measuring & reporting
Activity	Visitors	The number of people who are visitors (not registered members) to the community tool	Count Count per day Count per week Count per month
	Members	The number people who join the community	Count Count per day Count per week Count per month Count per geography Count per business unit
	Member activity	Number of active members The frequency of visits Time spent of each visits	Count of active members Number member visits per day Average time spent on each visit
	Conversations	Number of conversations started. Depth of conversation/ threads Length of posts Contributions	Count of new conversation/ threads. Count of the number of posts within a thread or conversation Word count Contribution per members Age of conversations

(continued)

Table 9.3 Continued

Category	Measure	Set a target	Measuring & reporting
Internal Community Value	Responsiveness	The speed with which posts and/or questions are responded to	Average time of a response
	Interest	The number of people who seek information about the community	Count
	Quality of dialog	Number of sentences in a message, Number of responses in a thread Number of new ideas	Randomized count
	Engagement and exploration	How many questions have been asked? Have members invited others to join?	Count
	Engagement	Are people getting involved? Do they know what they are doing?	Measure activity Poll on ease of involvement
	Generosity	What evidence is there of sharing? Have you seen people sharing ideas and offering to help?	Poll – ask people
Community Performance	Interest	Are people talking about the community in the wider organization? Have people heard about it?	Ask and record Narrative comments Run a poll on the company's intranet home page asking if people have heard of the community
	Awareness	Evidence that people are aware the community exists and what its scope, purpose, and theme are.	Discussion with stakeholders – what are they hearing? Record narrative
	Something new	A sense that the organization is open to experimentation and new ways of working	Test for buzz in the wider organization Carry out a poll on the organization's intranet. Have people heard of the community?

Stage 3 – coalescing

At this stage the focus of measuring needs to be on checking to see how well people have come together and are finding the workplace community a comfortable and easy place to work.

You should start to see a significant increase in the number of members. People will have been drawn to the purpose and will want to sign up, which is great. However, watch out for the number of members who drop in to see what's happening, and don't return! In line with the increasing membership, you will observe an increase in conversations as people become comfortable in making their first contribution. It is important that new members experience activity when they visit and anything you can do to reduce the threshold to contribution will help. It has surprised us many times how difficult it can be for an individual to share a thought or opinion in an online community, particularly if they are in a position of authority. However it is precisely when these people start to contribute that others will follow. You may want to monitor and measure the activity of these people as one segment of your community (Table 9.4).

Table 9.4   Stage 3 – coalescing: measurements

Category	Measure	Set a target	Measuring & reporting
Activity	Visitors	The number of people who are visitors (not registered members) to the community tool	Count Count per day Count per week Count per month
	Members	The number people who join the community	Count Count per day Count per week Count per month Count per geography Count per business unit
	Member activity	Number of active members The frequency of visits Time spent on each visit	Count of active members Number member visits per day Average time spent on each visit

(continued)

Table 9.4   Continued

Category	Measure	Set a target	Measuring & reporting
	Conversations	Number of conversations started.	Count of new conversation/threads.
		Depth of conversation/ threads	Count of the number of posts within a thread or conversation
		Length of posts	Word count
		Contributions	Contribution per members
			Age of conversations
Internal Community Value	Responsiveness	The speed with which posts and/or questions are responded to	Average time of a response to a post
	Interest	The number of people who seek information about the community	Count
	Quality of Dialog	Number of sentences in a message Number of responses in a thread Number of new ideas	Randomized count
	Engagement and exploration	How many questions have been asked? Have members invited others to join?	Count
	Level of comfort with community ways of working	What is good , OK, or not good. How are we doing? How is it for you?	Poll
	Nature of dialogue	Number of posts on topic Number of posts off topic	Sentiment analysis
	Belonging – people feel they have found their tribe	The extent to which people feel they belong in this community	Poll

(continued)

Table 9.4   Continued

Category	Measure	Set a target	Measuring & reporting
Community performance	Interest	Are people talking about the community in the wider organization Have people heard about it?	Ask and record Narrative comments Run a poll on the company's intranet home page asking if people have heard of the community
	Keeping connected – Connecting the community to the wider organization		

Stage 4 – discovery

During the discovery stage your focus for measurement needs to be on testing people's commitment to both the issue and the theme and also to a community way of working. This includes tracking what community members' are learning about the issues as well as what they are learning about themselves as community members.

Membership may no longer grow at the same rate. More importantly is that members are active and participating in the community. The initial enthusiasm for the community way of working may have subsided. The activity measures will show this lack of activity. Follow and measure where there is activity to understand the focus of the community and how this may be shifting. Are the members focusing on the original theme and purpose or has another topic emerged? Expect to see key contributors and opinion leaders emerge, and these should be clearly seen in your measures (Table 9.5).

Stage 5 – maturing

At this stage the focus of your measurement activities needs to be on confirming that the workplace community is adding value to the wider organization and its members. You also need to ensure that you are

Table 9.5   Stage 4 – discovery: measurements

Category	Measure	Set a target	Measuring & reporting
Activity	Visitors	The number of people who are visitors (not registered members) to the community tool	Count Count per day Count per week Count per month
	Members	The number people who join the community	Count Count per day Count per week Count per month Count per geography Count per business unit
	Member activity	Number of active members The frequency of visits The time spent on each visit	Count of active members Number member visits per day Average time spent on each visit Count of inactive members
	Conversations	Number of conversations started. Depth of conversation/threads Length of posts Contributions	Count of new conversation/threads. Count of the number of posts within a thread or conversation Word count Contribution per members Age of conversations
	Responsiveness	The speed with which posts and/or questions are responded to	Average time of a response
Internal Community Value	Interest	The number of people who seek information about the community	Count
	Quality of dialog	Number of Sentences in a message, Number of responses in a thread Number of new ideas	Randomized count
	Engagement and exploration	How many questions have been asked? Have members invited others to join?	Count

(continued)

Table 9.5   Continued

Category	Measure	Set a target	Measuring & reporting
	Knowledge assessment – are people learning and developing?		
Community performance	Interest	Are people talking about the community in the wider organization Have people heard about it?	Ask and record Narrative comments Run a poll on the company's intranet home page asking if people have heard of the community
	Identify outputs, products, services, change proposals etc. that can be attributed to the work of the community	Number of identified outputs, products, services, etc. Number of outputs integrated into company plans, strategy, innovations to a service etc.	Count - Product, services, change proposals in total Count those accepted and integrated into company business, ways of working etc. - develop impact measures to assess business value e.g. revenue, customer satisfaction, employee engagement etc.

both sustaining and maintaining the workplace community and that you are not unconsciously drifting. Things may change and new issues may emerge that mean you have to develop and extend your theme. It may also be that you find that your scope is more interconnected than you think. In which case you need to make a conscious choice, with community members to move your community in this direction. This of course means you will need to develop and review both your balanced scorecard and your metrics dashboard. Community members may well enjoy and relish the opportunity to widen their scope but beware of the desire to boil the ocean.

As the community grows up, while the activity measures will still be valid, there needs to be a shift to the more soft stuff – has a sense of belonging been created, do community members feel closely associated to the community? Has the focus of the community effort been lost? A huge increase in the number of unrelated conversations could indicate such drifting. Many, short and shallow threads will indicate that the community is chatting but not with any depth of purpose. Some of this is to be expected, but if this represents the majority of activity it will be time for an intervention (Table 9.6).

Table 9.6   Stage 5 – maturing: measurements

Category	Measure	Set a target	Measuring & reporting
Activity	Visitors	The number of people who are visitors (not registered members) to the community tool	Count Count per day Count per week Count per month
	Members	The number people who join the community	Count Count per day Count per week Count per month Count per geography Count per business unit
	Member activity	Number of active members The frequency of visits The time spent on each visit	Count of active members Number member visits per day Average time spent on each visit Number of inactive members
	Conversations	Number of conversations started. Depth of conversation/threads Length of posts Contributions	Count of new conversation/threads. Count of the number of posts within a thread or conversation Word count Contribution per members Age of conversations
	Responsiveness	The speed with which posts and/or questions are responded to	Average time of a response
	Interest	The number of people who seek information about the community	Count

(*continued*)

Table 9.6   Continued

Category	Measure	Set a target	Measuring & reporting
Internal Community Value	Quality of Dialog	Number of sentences in a message, Number of responses in a thread Number of new ideas	Randomized count
	Engagement and exploration	How many questions have been asked? Have members invited others to join?	Count
Community Performance	Interest	Are people talking about the community in the wider organization Have people heard about it?	Ask and record Narrative comments Run a poll on the company's intranet home page asking if people have heard of the community
	How do stakeholders view the outputs of the community?	% of positive feedback Set measure for perceived value of the community in the minds of stakeholders	Survey, interview, focus group etc.

Stage 6 – grown up

The measurement objectives for this stage are to see how far you have been able to translate the work of the community into outcomes for the wider organization and for community members.

The activity measures will have stabilized by this stage of the community. There may continue to be new members joining, and this is healthy. Members' status will have developed from novices or newbies to regulars and even key contributors as a result of the activity and contributions. People should, at this stage, be fairly comfortable with the community way of working. Contributions should be frequent, and the depth of conversation increased over earlier stages. Do pay attention to new members; do the measures show that that are contributing? It can be quite daunting, especially in a community of experts to be the new kid on the block, your novice contribution may not be well received. At this stage of community development, the community should have become extremely responsive, threads can 'catch fire' with responses, and requests for help can have almost real time responses (Table 9.7).

Table 9.7   Stage 6 – grown up: measurements

Category	Measure	Set a target	Measuring & reporting
Activity	Visitors	The number of people who are visitors (not registered members) to the community tool	Count Count per day Count per week Count per month
	Members	The number people who join the community	Count Count per day Count per week Count per month Count per geography Count per business unit
	Member activity	Number of active members The frequency of visits The time spent of each visits	Count of active members Number member visits per day Average time spent on each visit Number of inactive members
	Conversations	Number of conversations started. Depth of conversation/ threads Length of posts Contributions	Count of new conversation/threads. Count of the number of posts within a thread or conversation Word count Contribution per members Age of conversations
	Responsiveness	The speed with which posts and/or questions are responded to	Average time of a response
Internal Community Value	Interest	The number of people who seek information about the community	Count
	Quality of Dialog	Number of sentences in a message, Number of responses in a thread Number of new ideas	Randomized count

(continued)

Table 9.7   Continued

Category	Measure	Set a target	Measuring & reporting
	Engagement and exploration	How many questions have been asked? Have members invited others to join?	Count
	Interest	Are people talking about the community in the wider organization Have people heard about it?	Ask and record Narrative comments Run a poll on the company's intranet home page asking if people have heard of the community
	Community contributions are recognized in the wider organization	Number of times the community is positively referenced in the wider company Positive recognition in company performance management system for individual community contributions	Reviewing news articles, speeches, references, stories and anecdotes The number of company executives who wish to be associated with the community Number of times community referenced in performance reviews
Community Performance	Outcome measures (for example): • Number of customer problems solved • Reduced time to market of a product or service • Improved quality of product or service • Cost savings or cost avoidance • Improved innovation	Company specific	Company specific

Stage 7 – stewardship

Measurement activities at this stage all focus on giving voice to the community in the wider organization, ensuring it gets recognition for its work and as such is rewarded for its activities. It is also about stimulating discussion in the wider organization about the power of workplace communities to address issues in ways that would not be possible in the wider organization.

The measures during the stage will be very much focused on the community's performance, the value created for the wider organization. This stage of the community can last a long time, and your scorecard will be a good way to lightly monitor the activity. When the stage lasts years, you should expect to see fluctuations in membership and activity. This can reflect the general climate within the organization, and it will be quite natural for community members to leave. You may like to set threshold values in your scorecard to highlight certain conditions and act as a catalyst for when you will intervene (Table 9.8).

Table 9.8   Stage 7 – stewardship: measurements

Category	Measure	Set a target	Measuring & reporting
Activity	Visitors	The number of people who are visitors (not registered members) to the community tool	Count Count per day Count per week Count per month
	Members	The number people who join the community	Count Count per day Count per week Count per month Count per geography Count per business unit
	Member activity	Number of active members The frequency of visits The time spent of each visits	Count of active members Number member visits per day Average time spent on each visit Number of inactive members

(continued)

Table 9.8   Continued

Category	Measure	Set a target	Measuring & reporting
	Conversations	Number of conversations started. Depth of conversation/threads Length of posts Contributions	Count of new conversation/threads. Count of the number of posts within a thread or conversation Word count Contribution per members Age of conversations
	Responsiveness	The speed with which posts and/or questions are responded to	Average time of a response
Internal Community Value	Interest	The number of people who seek information about the community	Count
	Quality of dialog	Number of sentences in a message, Number of responses in a thread Number of new ideas	Randomized count
	Engagement and exploration	How many questions have been asked? Have members invited others to join?	Count
	Personal benefits and learning	What new skills, knowledge and connections do people have now as a consequence of being a member of the community	Questionnaire, sample interviews
Community Performance	Interest	Are people talking about the community in the wider organization Have people heard about it?	Ask and record Narrative comments Run a poll on the company's intranet home page asking if people have heard of the community

(continued)

Table 9.8   Continued

Category	Measure	Set a target	Measuring & reporting
Community Performance	Community contributions are recognized in the wider organization	Number of times the community is positively referenced in the wider company Positive recognition in company performance management system for individual community contributions	Reviewing news articles, speeches, references, stories and anecdotes The number of company executives who wish to be associated with the community Number of times community referenced in performance reviews
	Outcome measures (for example): • Number of customer problems solved • Reduced time to market of a product or service • Improved quality of product or service • Cost savings or cost avoidance • Improved innovation	Company specific	Company specific
	Impact on business strategy	Company specific	Company specific
	How is the community theme seen now, as a problem or an opportunity?	Company/theme specific	Company/theme specific

Stage 8 – transformation

At this stage measurement is all about confirming that the work of the community is over and complete. If the work of the community is complete then it is time either to close it or to support its transformation into something else.

Your community measures will tell you what you already know – the community is in transformation. You will have seen a reduction in activity, although people may still be visiting the community to access old materials. There will be very few if any new conversations or threads. The content of the interactions will primarily be based on the past not the future. Member numbers may not diminish, but active members certainly will. There will be a sense that the community has done what it was created for, time to close it, or to find a new purpose.

The transformation stage can also occur when there is a significant change to the community. Again the measurements and your scorecard will clearly indicate that this has happened. Be careful not act too quickly to close your community – it may be that it's vacation season! Although it is far more likely for a community leader to continue to keep the community 'alive', at least open, even they know and the measurements will clearly indicate it has come to an end (Table 9.9).

Table 9.9   Stage 8 – transformation: measurements

Category	Measure	Set a Target	Measuring & Reporting
Activity	Visitors	The number of people who are visitors (not registered members) to the community tool	Count Count per day Count per week Count per month
	Members	The number people who join the community	Count Count per day Count per week Count per month Count per geography Count per business unit
	Member activity	Number of active members The frequency of visits The time spent of each visits	Count of active members Number member visits per day Average time spent on each visit

(continued)

Table 9.9 Continued

Category	Measure	Set a Target	Measuring & Reporting
Activity	Conversations	Number of conversations started. Depth of conversation/threads Length of posts Contributions	Count of new conversation/threads. Count of the number of posts within a thread or conversation Word count Contribution per members Age of conversations
	Responsiveness	The speed with which posts and/or questions are responded to	Average time of a response
	After action review	Capture a number of learnings Produce a number of stories Publicize	AAR process
Internal community Value	Interest	The number of people who seek information about the community	Count
	Quality of dialog	Number of sentences in a message, Number of responses in a thread Number of new ideas	Randomized count
	Engagement and exploration	How many questions have been asked? Have members invited others to join?	Count
	Learning review	Number people who are willing to undertake Quality of narrative comments	Poll Narrative comments

(continued)

Table 9.9 Continued

Category	Measure	Set a Target	Measuring & Reporting
Community performance	Interest	Are people talking about the community in the wider organization? Have people heard about it?	Ask and record Narrative comments Run a poll on the company's intranet home page asking if people have heard of the community
	Community contributions are recognized in the wider organization	Number of times the community is positively referenced in the wider company Positive recognition in company performance management system for individual community contributions	Reviewing news articles, speeches, references, stories and anecdotes The number of company executives who wish to be associated with the community Number of times community referenced in performance reviews
	Outcome measures (for example): • Number of customer problems solved • Reduced time to market of a product or service • Improved quality of product or service • Cost savings or cost avoidance • Improved innovation	Company specific	Company specific
	Impact on business strategy	Company specific	Company specific
	How is the community theme seen now, as a problem or an opportunity?	Company/theme specific	Company/theme specific
	Recognition	Kudos, awards, badges, 'likes' etc.	Count

(continued)

Table 9.9   Continued

Category	Measure	Set a Target	Measuring & Reporting
	Acceptance of community ways of working as a contribution to organization performance	Have default positions changed to include community ways of working? How often is a community way of working chosen over and above another way of working?	Count, the number of communities instigates in any one year Number of community roles published and recruited to Embedded in the perform management system etc

Summary

The measurement approach we have applied for workplace communities consists of two elements: the ROI plan and the workplace community scorecard.

The ROI plan helps establish the value proposition from the outset and sells the community idea and ways-of-working to stakeholders and relevant parties. It includes eight questions where you provide the answers and measurements that apply specifically to your workplace community. In our example (see below), we have added leading indicators to pinpoint what success may look like. The leading indicator is your threshold or the target you want to surpass as your workplace community develops and starts to execute.

In addition, the ROI plan supports determining the degree of success at the various stages of its development and as the community moves towards its final stages. At this point, you analyze metrics gathered in all stages to check how the community performance stacks up against your original ROI plan. The final ROI calculation is part of the lessons learned, it is an output on how the community performed overall. The final ROI calculation will also help you to understand how accurate and relevant your ROI plan was as decision parameter and direction guidance.

The second element of the measurement approach is the workplace community scorecard. It contains three categories: 1) activity metrics, 2) internal community value, and 3) community performance as judged by the wider organization. For each category, there is a range of metrics that applies to each of the individual stages of the workplace community life cycle.

From the three categories, we suggest that you tailor the scorecard of metrics to your specific needs and reporting requirements. Again, you may want to include leading indicators for success as in the example provided. Leading indicators will help you to determine what immediate steps to take to change things in the short or longer term. The work community scorecard is a tool for you to manage the activity, value and performance of the community on an ongoing basis as well as to determine success at the end. Our advice is to keep the scorecard simple with a set of essential metrics for each category and each stage. You can add metrics along the way if you miss anything essential or get specific measurement inquiries. The exercise is not about keeping the scorecard alive, but about helping you to make the workplace community engaging and value-adding!

The ROI example (on the next page) is based on a scenario in which a product is currently selling well on the German market and will now be introduced to the Indian market. The company has divided India into four sales regions. The global product manager and the product manager for the German market would like to establish a workplace community to explore how this product might be localized and successfully launched in the huge Indian market. They believe there are massive potential sales for the product, but are aware that they need local knowledge and understand if this is to be realized. They will need people from many parts of the organization including; global sales and marketing, technology, and supply chain experts, as well as their Indian colleagues, especially those most familiar with local market conditions in the various parts of India. The targeted workplace community size is 100 employees. The community should furthermore be as diverse as possible and representative of the targeted potential consumer base in India. The intention is to position the workplace community as a new way of going to market and appeal to colleagues' discretionary effort to join as well as to use traditional ways of recruiting key individuals to participate. The intention is to tap into as much local frontline knowledge and understanding as possible and to use this to position the product and shape the go-to-market (GTM) activities.

The process of applying the ROI plan is to create the plan and then to check progress against the plan, at the various stages of the workplace community life cycle, using real results, and ultimately to demonstrate how well the ROI plan was achieved (Table 9.10) (Table 9.11).

Table 9.10 Return on investment (ROI) plan – example

ROI question	Return on investment (ROI) plan – example: product launch India		
	Your answer	Leading indicator	How to measure
What you wish to achieve	Replication of success with product X on market A to market B. This is a huge and risky undertaking and to solve it in a workplace community will bring fresh ideas and identify more opportunities/mitigate more of the risks.	Net promoter score positive in piloting and subsequently. Sales volumes better than with traditional approach. Risk mitigation proves accurate.	Consumer feedback. Sales volumes
What the organization wishes to achieve	Successful launch of product X in market B which is a very large, diverse, and a difficult market to enter	As above	As above
Importance to me	Try out a new way of solving a business challenge, getting my workplace community to reflect consumers in both markets	Harvest at least ten ideas per day, good spread across life & career stages among members	Targets for dialogues and insights per day/month, diversity of participants
Importance to the organization	Giving everyone the chance to be a leader and using crowd sourcing to solve a real business challenge. Can become competitive advantage for future GTM activities.	30% of participants take leadership at some stage, harvesting of ideas (as above)	Workplace community scorecard targets
If we do nothing?	Product launch may be less successful, missed market opportunities	Product breaks even faster than with traditional approach	Breakeven analysis

(continued)

Table 9.10 Continued

	Return on investment (ROI) plan – example: product launch India		
ROI question	**Your answer**	**Leading indicator**	**How to measure**
How to evaluate impact and outcomes?	Consumer feedback positive, net promoter score. Product launch targets better than with traditional approach. Development for employees. Emerging leaders. Workplace community scorecard.	Positive Net Promoter Score (NPS), sales volumes follow plan, employees see link to development (70% favorable), 50% of appointed target group participate	NPS targets, sales volume targets, promote as part of 70/20/10 development, targeted appointment of opinion leaders and experts
How the community ranks against competing priorities?	A calculated risk. Possible game changer: New work environment, freeing itself from corporate culture, values, customs, and ways of working.	Opportunities 2X risks	List of opportunities (coming from all ROI questions) and risks
Why should people give discretionary effort to this community?	Will appeal to employees wanting to try something new, curiosity, creativity, and contribution, helping to build and grow something they can take real pride in. Opportunity to influence the product and GTM activities.	70% are in favor of giving their discretionary effort	A quick poll with opinion leaders, experts and other relevant stakeholders

Table 9.11   Workplace community scorecard

A: Activity	Workplace community scorecard							
	1. Initiation	2. Potential	3. Coalescing	4. Discovery	5. Maturing	6. Grown up	7. Stewardship	8. Transformation
Visitors	50% of target audience	75% of remaining audience	50% of remaining audience	As many as possible	As many as possible	As many as possible	As many as possible	Few weekly visitors
Members (visitors who join community)	80% of visitors; 50% of targeted opinion leaders and experts join	80% of visitors	50% of visitors	Member level stable	Member level stable	Member level stable	Member level stable	Members start to leave
Member activity	>80% of members are active	>80% of members are active	>60% of members are active	>50% of members are active	>80% of members are active	>80% of members are active	>50% of members are active	<20% of members are active
Conversations	10 new conversations/day; 50% of conversations get replies	20 new conversations/day; 50% of conversations get replies	10 new conversations/day; 50% of conversations get replies	10 new conversations/day; 75% of conversations get replies, focus on innovation	Stable level of conversations and replies with focus on execution	Increased focus on execution	Focus on lessons learned, on a personal and community level	Few new conversations
Responsiveness	Posts/questions are responded to within same day	Posts/questions are responded to within same day	Posts/questions are responded to within same day	Response rules and alerts are agreed and kept	Response rules and alerts are agreed and kept	Response rules and alerts are agreed and kept	Posts/questions are responded to within same week	Ad-hoc

(continued)

Table 9.11 Continued

Workplace community scorecard								
B: Internal Community Value	1. Initiation	2. Potential	3. Coalescing	4. Discovery	5. Maturing	6. Grown up	7. Stewardship	8. Transformation
Quality of dialogue/insights/hot topics	Min 3 replies to a conversation; 1 new idea/day	Min 5 replies to a conversation; 2 new idea/day	Min 3 replies to a conversation; 1 new idea/day	Min 5 replies to a conversation; 2 new idea/day	Min 5 replies to a conversation	Min 5 replies to a conversation	Quantity diminishes, quality stays	Thank you, good bye notes
Engagement, exploration	50% members invited others to join; 30 questions asked/week	50% members invited others to join; 50 questions asked/week	50% members invited others to join; 30 questions asked/week	Member level stable; 50 questions asked/week	Member level stable; 50 questions asked/week	Member level stable; 50 questions asked/week	Member level stable; less frequent Q&As	Members recruiting for other tasks
Generosity		Predominantly positive wording; publish the scorecard	Predominantly positive wording; publish the scorecard	People contribute with ideas and offer help	People contribute with ideas and offer help	People contribute with ideas and offer help	Predominantly positive wording; publish the scorecard	Publish the final scorecard and ROI
Diversity, comfort, sense of belonging	Review of members how reflect markets and consumers, diversity criteria		Comments on community achievement, words such as we/the team, jokes	Team spirit permeates; we are proud of what we do here – 80% in favor	We are in action!	We are in action!	After-action activities	We achieved this!
Knowledge sharing, learnings	Dedicated members take responsibility for documentation library; dedicated members take responsibility for idea harvesting	All members use documentation library and utilize idea groupings/themes	All members use documentation library and utilize idea groupings/themes	Give/take equation; 30% of members have assumed leader role; harvesting & evaluating ideas	Prioritizing ideas & outlining actions	Executing tasks	Feedback from community members; link to own development	Members come back for materials and testimonials

C: Community Performance	1. Initiation	2. Potential	3. Coalescing	4. Discovery	5. Maturing	6. Grown up	7. Stewardship	8. Transformation
Interest from the wider organization	10% of wider organization has heard about this community (poll on intranet)	20% of wider organization has heard about this community (poll on intranet)	Stable level of interest	Stable level of interest	Stable level of interest	30% of wider organization has heard about this community (poll on intranet)	30% of wider organization has heard about this community (poll on intranet)	
Awareness	Stakeholders in support	Managers and HR start to talk about it	Managers and HR keep talking about it	Managers and HR keep talking about it	Managers and HR keep talking about it	Managers and HR keep talking about it	HR helps to document best practice	
Something new			Recognition in Leadership Teams	Recognition in Leadership Teams	Recognition in Leadership Teams	List deliverables, what was accomplished and how it was done	Best practice is shared with leaders	
Outputs	Document repository; ideas, conversations, hot topics	Document repository; ideas, conversations, hot topics	Gross list of ideas	Idea catalogue with prioritization and actions	Action plan; how do stakeholders view deliverables?	Recognition from the wider organization; ROI model revisited	ROI final calculation	
Impact on strategy								Summary of hot topics, opportunities and problems

chapter 10

Transformation

Introduction

In this book we have introduced you to the key elements and components we believe you need to initiate, launch and support a successful workplace community. Here we want to provide you with a brief summary of what we have shared, along with our final thoughts and reflections.

Our aim with this book has been to keep things as practical as possible. By doing so we hope we have encouraged you to dip your toe into the world of workplace communities and give it a go! If you do, not only will you be developing your own skills and capabilities we believe you will also be offering your organization the opportunity to unleash untapped potential and the chance of becoming a truly twenty-first century workplace!

Workplace communities can, have and will emerge within organizations wherever there is the shared intent, belief, resources, preferences, and a positive approach to risk. Workplace communities will typically adapt to the interests of their members and in this regard are more sensitive to the environment than traditional organizational structures. Workplace communities provide the ability to tap into and benefit from the collective intelligence of your organization, to engage a large number of people and to inspire them to go above and beyond.

For a while now you have been thinking that there must be other ways of getting work done. Your organization is doing fairly well and overall you are happy with things. However you cannot help but think that 'fairly' is not good enough. Is working for a fairly good organization what you want your personal legacy to be? Or is there something else? When you have retired and are sitting having tea and talking to others about how you spent your working life, you want to be able to share with them stories about how you made a difference and how you were able to raise not only your game but that of others in the workplace. Having read this book your eyes have been opened to the fact that there might be something different you can try and experiment with – workplace communities. You can think of any number of themes, topics and issues that a workplace community might help with. It's now just a case of getting started, having the courage to think differently and to approach those who you need to get on board and begin the process of workplace community-building. What you need, before you close this book and get on with it, is a short and brief summary that pulls together what you have learnt and gives you a place to start.

A place to start

The diagram below provides a handy summary of the critical building blocks that need to be in place for your workplace community to flourish and succeed. It also shows what can happen if they are not in place. We have covered these in much more detail in the various chapters of the book and also provided you with a range of tools and techniques to help you make sure you can put them in place. The figure below provides a handy reminder (Figure 10.1).

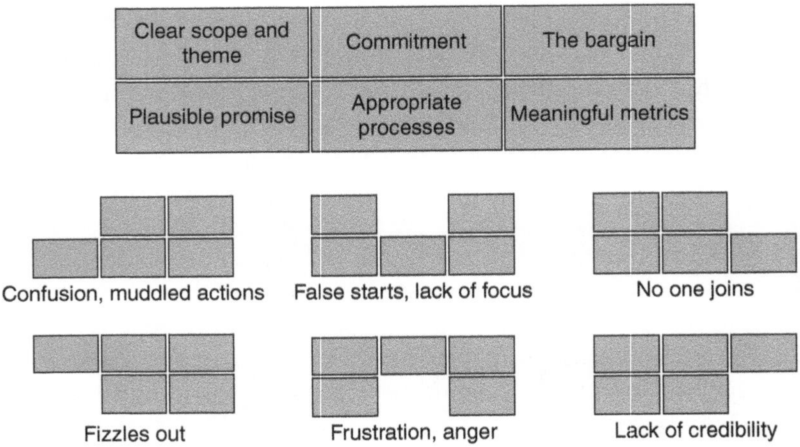

Clear scope and theme	Commitment	The bargain
Plausible promise	Appropriate processes	Meaningful metrics

Confusion, muddled actions · False starts, lack of focus · No one joins

Fizzles out · Frustration, anger · Lack of credibility

FIG 10.1 Workplace community – what can go wrong

Clarity of scope and purpose

You need to spend time thinking through your intentions for your workplace community and developing a compelling theme that will inspire people to join and contribute. Be clear on the scope of the community and as interesting things start to happen, be ready to see as this shift and develop. It might extend into areas you never would have thought possible. It also might retreat into something much smaller than you imagine. Once community members start to engage with your theme and make it their own, their collective intelligence and action is bound to have an impact on it.

As the workplace community initiator you need to ensure that the community does not go so far off topic that it starts to lose its relevance and community members at best stop contributing and at worst start leaving. So, for example, a community that has been set up to explore entry into new and emerging markets that suddenly starts working on how to recruit a new CEO will need some kind of intervention! However, if the topic shifts to looking at talent management, the need for specific skills related to the new markets and how to get them, then by using your judgment and what you have learnt from this book, you will be able to explore if this is a key element within the scope, theme and purpose of the community. Be prepared to be surprised and be prepared to have patience and to not make snap decisions.

Without clarity and scope you will end up with confusion and muddled actions within your workplace community. Community members will not be clear on what is expected of them and you will find it hard, if not impossible, to make sense of things and harvest anything positive from the experience.

Resist the urge to unilaterally announce that we are a community! Remember that the community will exist when the members behave like a community not because the initiator says it is one.

Commitment

Workplace communities require commitment on both your part as the initiator and also as well as on the part of community members. In our experience, and certainly at initiation and through the early stages, most of the work that is needed will happen through discretionary rather than mandated effort. At these stages you may not even be fully supported by the wider organization. As initiator you need to really believe in what you are doing and approach it with a committed spirit of inquiry and exploration. The initiator together with key contributors will often form the core of the workplace community, especially in the early stages, and it will be through their actions and contribution that others will be attracted to become members.

The issue of organization commitment is an interesting one. We have given you suggestions and tools to help with this, but we would suggest that at this early stage you do not expect too much. In our experience, we have seen at worst total disinterest and at best benign neglect on the part of stakeholders. Using this book will help you to engage with them in ways we hope will help you get them on board. However very often they will only get interested in what you are doing when they start to see something happening. Your job, as an initiator, is to manage their interest and expectations in ways that don't let them get in the way of what is happening. Get them engaged and involved. Even invite them to join in!

There will be hurdles on the road but with a positive spirit of inquiry these hurdles can be overcome. The worst that might happen is that nothing happens. But at least you will have done something! The best that can happen is that you will have connected many people across your organization and discovered things you never could have discovered on your own. You will have brought about real and lasting change. The wider organization will have benefited through getting a resolution to a conundrum that it has been trying to resolve, perhaps for many years. It will now have access to a group of talented people who no longer feel trapped by their silos or positions and who can now see the organization 'in the round' and know they have a new way of contributing. You will also have people, workplace community members, who experienced a new way of working and who feel more engaged and committed to their roles, their development and the wider organization. You will have built your own and others' capabilities and capacity.

Without commitment you are likely to find that you have a number of false starts. It looks like things have got going and then they stop or get stuck. Only to start again as some community members try to initiate something, but fail to gain traction. In essence people will lack focus and will experience feelings of being scattered and unsure of what being a community member is all about.

The bargain

People will not want to engage with or join your workplace community unless the bargain is clear. They need to understand what is expected of them and what they can expect for their commitment. As we have explored in this book, this is not about a normal set of rewards, the usual suspects of position, pay and incentives. It is more to do with a wide range of things; including, recognition, being able to contribute, learning something new, feeling engaged and involved, working on something important, connecting with new people and truly feeling part of and engaged with something.

In essence the bargain is about community members being given the opportunity of working and contributing to something that is important to them.

If your bargain is not clear then people are unlikely to join. They won't know what is in it for them, what they can hope to achieve both personally and professionally. It may seem obvious to say this, but a workplace community is nothing more than a good idea if you cannot establish a bargain that will attract and retain members!

Plausible promise

Plausible promise is what connects people in the community. If the bargain is why people want to become members of your community, it is the plausible promise that will encourage them to start and continue to work together.

If you cannot find positive ways of building plausible promise and making it explicit, your workplace community is likely to fizzle out. You may have a successful launch, but if the promise of connecting with people to achieve something new and exciting cannot be fulfilled then those people are unlikely to stay for very long, let alone contribute.

Workplace communities need a plausible promise, something that is plausible, reasonable, achievable, and even probable. If the plausible promise is interpreted as a mission impossible it is highly likely that the community will fail to gain traction, people will feel they are being asked to contribute to boiling the ocean. Keep the plausible promise realistic.

Appropriate processes

When we use the term appropriate processes remember how we explored in previous chapters that workplace communities tend to be loosely based groups of people who have come together in a non-hierarchical and non-regimented way. However you do need to have in place a number of processes to enable this coming together to happen. These function as a guide and support to enable people to contribute and work together.

We explored the importance of having clear and appropriate processes for the evolutionary stages of your workplace community. Processes include:

- Plans for initiation and launch
- Process for knowledge management
- Support for the transition between stages
- Appropriate tools and technology to connect members
- Routines and rituals specific to the community
- Intervention tools and techniques to help keep the community moving forward
- Shared ways for harvesting ideas and stimulating innovation and creativity

As your workplace community matures it will become increasingly self-managing. However this does not mean it won't need recognizable processes to help it function. These processes can only fall into the background, where they should be, once community members understand what they are and how to best access and use them.

Effective processes that people understand and feel comfortable with mean that community members can focus on the issue and the topic in hand and not be distracted by things not working or be confused about how to get things done. If community members are wasting time, energy and effort and being distracted by things outside of the community's theme, it will be much harder to achieve the outcomes you and your community members desire. People are also likely to become irritated and feel it is impossible to get things done.

A lack of appropriate process will lead to frustration and anger on the part of community members. If people cannot trust the processes then they are likely to lose trust in the whole idea of workplace communities.

A community facilitator role is usually responsible for maintaining the process of the community. In larger workplace communities this can become a full-time role or even require several people to perform it. Don't underestimate the need for a facilitator especially in the early stages of community development.

Meaningful metrics

Metrics and measurement of results are one of the ways in which your workplace community stays connected to the wider organization. Having a credible set of metrics and an explicit plan for return on investment is one of the ways in which you will be able to engage with stakeholders.

Key stakeholders may initially be sceptical about this new way of working and require a high degree of convincing that you are not wasting people's time and distracting them from work that needs to be done. Good metrics will help community members engage with their stakeholders. It will also help them to understand and track how their work, energy and effort is contributing to the overall direction and success of your workplace community.

Intuition is great and your sense that a workplace community will make a difference is wonderful. Your intuition will help drive your enthusiasm and help you to connect with others and encourage them to get involved. However intuition in today's organization is not enough on its own. You need to be able to back it up and support it in ways that the wider organization recognizes and accepts. This will be through developing an upfront plan for return on investment and having a credible score card of metrics. In our Chapter on measurement and Meaning we have provided you with a process for developing a measurement strategy as well as examples of metrics that you can easily adapt and develop to help you with developing your own return on investment plan.

A lack of metrics or poor metrics and a weak measurement strategy means that your community is likely to struggle to achieve any kind of credibility in the organization. It may end up being seen as an interesting hobby, something you are playing with, but not something that is likely to make a difference or a contribution to the future success of the organization.

Evolution versus revolution in the workplace

Community ways of working are neither inherently revolutionary nor evolutionary in terms of organization development. They can be both! You may simply choose to initiate and launch a workplace community to address a specific issue and once that is over, close it down. On the other hand you may decide that launching a workplace community could be part of a bigger organizational development initiative to help the wider organization bring about a greater transformation in its ways of working. Providing the opportunity for the organization to explore how moving away from the 'default position' of hierarchy can bring new possibilities and exciting opportunities. Workplace communities can also be used as levers for business transformation and cultural change.

We believe that in today's organizations and with a workforce increasingly comprised of employees who are social media literate, we need to have a serious rethink about how work is carried out. Employees who are used to collaborating outside the workplace, to contributing and having their generosity rewarded, will increasingly have an expectation of something similar in the workplace.

We are entering an era when the contrast between how people live their day-to-day lives, and then experience life in the workplace has never been greater. We believe that what you have learnt through reading this book can help you to bridge this divide. By experimenting and moving fast you will be able to work on your own personal development and on your organization's business competitive advantage, developing new skills and abilities and helping others to do the same.

Coming to the end

Just as with the final stage in our model describing the life cycle of community evolution, it is now time for this book to transform and change! We have covered all that we intended to cover and believe we have provided you with a practical introduction and guide to establishing and supporting successful workplace communities.

We have included a number of tools, checklists and interventions that you may use to assess and maintain the health of a workplace community. We have also helped you to position your workplace community within the boundaries of a wider organization in such a way that it will flourish. And we have positioned workplace communities as a recognizable way of working. Placing it on par with the hierarchy, program and project mode and intrapreneurial ways of working. We hope we have encouraged you to see that how you get work done is a choice and not a default position. By making choices and giving yourself the opportunity to select a way of working which will bring the kind of outcomes you are looking for, you raise the possibility of creating the kind of workplace in which people feel able to give of their best and be rewarded for it.

Communities are one of the oldest forms of human organization. During the industrial era other forms of organization became the default as they offered predictability, scale and efficiency as humans worked with their hands on typically repetitive tasks in factories and in agriculture. As we move beyond the industrial era into the digital and Internet age, workplace communities offer us the possibility to accomplish our organizational goals and objectives through new ways of working; ways that engage people, mobilize human capability and tap into the collective intelligence of our organizations. You'll be amazed at the results of a workplace community.

Go on have a go!

Bibliography and Additional Resources

Bibliography

Anderson, C. (2006) *The Long Tail*. New York City, NY, USA: Hyperion.

Center for Civic Engagement. *The Asset-Based Community Development Institute, School of Education and Social Policy*, Northwestern University, Evanston II, USA.

Gratton, L. (2007) *Hot Spots, Why Some Companies Buzz with Energy and Innovation and Others Don't*. Harlow, UK: Prentice Hall.

Peters, T. and Austen, A. (1994) *Passion for Excellence: The Leadership Difference*. New York, NY, USA: Harper Collins Business.

Plotkin, B. (2008) *Nature and the Human Soul*. Novato CA, USA: New World Library.

Taylor, F. (1911) *The Principles of Scientific Management*. New York City, NY, USA: Harper Brothers.

Titmus, R. (1970) *The Gift Relationship: From Human Blood to Social Policy*. New York, NY, USA: New Press.</REF>

Tuckman, B. (1965) 'Developmental Sequences in Small Groups', *Psychological Bulletin*, Vol. 63, pp. 384–399.

Turner, J. R. (2009) *The Handbook of Project Based Management – Leading Strategic Change in Organisations*. Columbus OH, USA: McGraw-Hill.

Wenger, E. W., McDermott, R. and Snyder W. M. (2002) *Cultivating Communities of Practice*. Boston, MA, USA: Harvard Business School Press.

Additional Resources

Adair, J. (1986) *Effective Teambuilding*. Basingstoke, Hampshire, UK: Pan Macmillian.

Bacon, J. (2012) *The Art of Community: Building the New Age of Participation.* Sebastopol, CA, USA: O'Reilly.

Block, P. (2008) *Community, the Structure of Belonging.* San Francisco, CA, USA: Berrett-Koehler Inc.

De Board, R. (1978) *The Psychoanalysis of Organisations.* London, UK: Tavistock/Routledge.

Drucker, P. (2007) *Management Challenges for the 21st Century.* New York City, NY, USA: Harper Collins.

Godin, S. (2008) *Tribes.* London, UK: Piatkus.

Gossieaux, F. and Moran, E. (2010) *The Hyper Social Organization.* Columbus, OH, USA: McGraw Hill.

Gratton, L. (2011) *The Shift.* London, UK: Harper Collins.

Hamel, G. (2007) *The Future of Management.* Boston, MA, USA: Harvard Business School Press.

Hansen, M. T. (2009) *Collaboration, How Leaders Avoid the Traps, Build Common Ground and Reap Big Results.* Boston, MA, USA: Harvard Business Press.

Holmes, P. and Devane, T. (2007) *The Change Handbook: The Definitive Resource for Todays Best Methods for Engaging Whole Systems.* San Francisco, CA, USA: Berrett-Koehler.

Kohn, M. (2008) *Trust – Self Interest and the Common Good.* Oxford, UK: Oxford University Press.

Lencioni, J. B. (2002) *The Five Dysfunctions of a Team: A Leadership Fable.* San Francisco, CA, USA: Jossey Bass.

MacKenzie, G. (1998) *Orbiting the Giant Hairball: A Corporate Fools Guide to Surviving with Grace.* New York City, NY, USA: Viking.

Maitland, A. and Thomson, P. (2014) *Future Work, Changing Organisation Culture of the New World of Work.* Basingstoke, Hampshire UK: Palgrave Macmillan.

McAfee, A. (2009) *Enterprise 2.0, New Collaborative Tools for Your Organisations Toughest Challenge.* Boston, MA, USA: Harvard Business Press.

Senge, P. (2006) *The Fifth Discipline – The Art and Practice of the Learning Organization.* New York City, NY, USA: Doubleday.

Shirky, C. (2008) *Here Comes Everybody.* New York City NY, USA: Penguin Press.

Tapscott, D. and Williams, A. D. (2008) *Wikinomics.* New York City, NY, USA: Penguin Group.

Von Oech, R. (2008) *A Whack on the Side of the Head.* New York City, NY, USA: Warner Books.

Bibliography and Additional Resources

Weinberger, D. (2008) *Everything Is Miscellaneous: The Power of the New Digital Disorder*. New York City, NY USA: Henry Holt.

Williams, I. (1999) *Dialogue and the Art of Thinking Together: A Pioneering Approach to Communicating in Business and in Life*. New York City NY, USA: Doubleday.

About the Authors

Ian Gee

Ian has worked in Organization Development (OD) for the past 30 years. He started his career working for UK public services before moving to the Office for Public Management, a boutique consultancy based in London. Here the focus of his work, in the UK and overseas, was on OD to support public sector and not-for-profit organizations in achieving and maximizing the social results of their work.

In 1996, Ian joined Shell International's global OD team as a Senior OD Practitioner. Whilst with Shell he led a number of global change projects with a focus on systemic change as well as organization effectiveness.

In May 2006 Ian moved to Nokia Corp and in 2007 became Director of OD and led a team of consultants delivering services across Nokia businesses around the world. Ian's work for Nokia included designing and leading the renewal of the Nokia Way, developing and implementing Nokia's approach to Enterprise 2.0. Web 2.0 and the Net Gen. Ian has also led work on the integration of mergers and acquisitions in Nokia, ensuring on-going employee engagement and making sure that there was an appropriate cultural fit to maximize the value of the acquisition in the most human way. Prior to leaving Nokia Ian co-led a year-long study into what constitutes best practice for change and OD in the emerging markets.

In 2012 Ian decided to set up on his own and is now running Edgelands Consultancy offering OD consultancy services to both the Private and Public/NGO sectors. Ian is also Co-founder and Director of Albany OD.

Ian has a great deal of interest in how the nature of change is changing and also in the relationship between human resources (HR) and entrepreneurs.

Ian is regularly asked to speak at national and international conferences on issues to do with change and OD.

Ian is known for the innovation, creativity and humour he brings to his work supported by a deep commitment to implementation, with the focus on the achievement of outcomes.

Matthew Hanwell

With over 20 years of experience in the area of people-centric information technology in high-tech industries, Matthew has been responsible for developing and driving HR systems and technology, web-based services, analytics, and new ways of working focussing on community, collaboration and social media.

Matthew worked at Nokia from 1997 to 2012, where he held various positions within HR and IT with global responsibility including HR Director Community and Social Media. His time at Nokia was spent developing and driving forward HR and people-centric technology in support of business needs; from implementing a global Enterprise Resource Planning (SAP R/3 – software from SAP AG), through developing a portfolio of web-based solutions and services (performance management, compensation management, recruiting, reporting and analytics), corporate intranet development and a portfolio of social media and collaboration capabilities.

Prior to Nokia, Matthew spent 11 years at Digital Equipment Corporation, in various project management, and HRIT roles, finally having the role of European HRIS manager.

Matthew has been a speaker and panellist at many international events and conferences, and has presented on HR technology, HR analytics and the use of collaboration and social media capabilities.

Matthew lives in Finland, is married and has five children.

Both Ian and Matthew regularly blog about issues to do with HR, OD and change management at The Illusion of Work (www.theillusionof-work.wordpress.com)

Index

Printed and bound in Great Britain by
CPI Group (UK) Ltd, Croydon, CR0 4YY